Thomas Cook

Programme and Itineraries of Cook's Grand Excursions to

Europe

Season 1881

Thomas Cook

Programme and Itineraries of Cook's Grand Excursions to Europe
Season 1881

ISBN/EAN: 9783744788540

Printed in Europe, USA, Canada, Australia, Japan

Cover: Foto ©Andreas Hilbeck / pixelio.de

More available books at **www.hansebooks.com**

Programme & Itineraries of Cook's GRAND EXCURSIONS TO EUROPE

Under the Management of

Thos Cook & Son,
LUDGATE CIRCUS LONDON

AND

261 Broadway, New York.

SEASON 1881

G. A. BARATTONI, MANAGER OF THE AMERICAN BUSINESS

GUIDE BOOKS.

The following Guide Books can be obtained at any of the offices of *THOS. COOK & SON,* or will be forwarded by mail on receipt of price.

PROGRAMME AND ITINERARIES

OF

COOK'S

GRAND EXCURSIONS TO EUROPE,

Season 1881,

VISITING ALL CHIEF POINTS OF INTEREST IN

Ireland, Scotland, England, Holland,

BELGIUM, GERMANY,

SWITZERLAND, ITALY. FRANCE,

ETC., ETC..

Leaving NEW YORK by

Cunard, Inman and Anchor Lines of Steamers,

ON

APRIL 27th, JUNE 11th and JULY 2d, 1881.

CONTAINING SPECIALLY ENGRAVED MAP OF EUROPE.

— ◆◆ —

UNDER THE MANAGEMENT OF

THOMAS COOK & SON,

Originators of the World-renowned Tourist and Excursion System, (Established 1841,) and only successful Conductors of Tours and Excursions to all parts of the Globe ; specially appointed by His Royal Highness the Prince of Wales, Sole Passenger Agents to the Royal British Commission, Vienna 1873, Philadelphia 1876, and Paris 1878.

— ◆◆ —

CHIEF OFFICE, LUDGATE CIRCUS, LONDON.

CHIEF AMERICAN OFFICE,

261 Broadway, New York.

C. A. BARATTONI, Manager of the American Business.

CONTENTS.

--- • ---

INTRODUCTORY NOTES.

At the completion of the fortieth year of this unique business, and in placing before the American public the Programme of our Traveling arrangements to Europe for the Season 1881, we again take the opportunity of defining our position as the **Originators and Promoters of the European Tourist and Excursion System, and the only successful Conductors of Tours to all parts of the Globe.**

Forty years is a very short period in the history of nations, but it is seldom that the originator of a system (such as our Tourist and Excursion system has proved to be) lives to see his ideas worked out and extended until they become universally adopted by all classes of society, in all parts of the world, as is the case with MR. THOMAS COOK, and whose original plans are now being carried out on a more extensive scale by his son, MR. JOHN M. COOK, the present Managing partner of our firm.

Out of the hundreds of thousands who have traveled under our arrangements during the past years, we can easily understand that a very small percentage are aware that the present extensive business originated with a cheap excursion of 11 miles in distance at the fare of 25 cents per passenger, and that from that small beginning the present unique institution has grown. We are also aware that there are thousands of persons in America who wish to travel, and who may have heard of the name of COOK, but who have little or no idea of the enormous extent of our business, the universal facilities at our command, or the soundness and stability of our financial position and undertakings.

As the founders of this peculiar system, established in 1841, we are the pioneers and leaders of tourist arrangements in all parts of the world. It is a well-known fact that our firm has been successful, and therefore it is not surprising that imitators should spring up on all sides, copying our system as much as possible, and placing it before the public as their own. Of course, it is impossible to patent or copyright such a system, nor the numerous novel ideas which we have brought before the public year after year.

The unrivaled facilities, however, which we are in the position to offer to travelers, we are confident will be, as in former years, fully recognized and appreciated by the American traveling public, and it should be distinctly understood that THOS. COOK & SON *are the* ONLY *persons in America advertising traveling facilities to Europe and other parts of the world, who are able to, and do, carry out their own arrangements, and that no other persons in America advertising tours to Europe and the East possess similar facilities, but are entirely dependent upon some one else in Europe to carry out the same for them.*

PERSONALLY CONDUCTED PARTIES.

Our annual parties to Europe are now so well known to Americans, and so well understood, that it is not necessary for us to say much about them; suffice it to say, that over 1,500 ladies and gentlemen, representing almost every State in the Union, have visited Europe, in connection with our parties; and we have no doubt they have reported to thousands of friends their opinions as to the manner in which THOS. COOK & SON carry out their contracts, and the advantages they have gained by traveling under our arrangements with such associated parties, composed of people gathered together from all parts of the States, for the object of obtaining rest, relaxation and new vigor.

We have received very flattering testimonials from many of the members of these parties, and we know that many lasting friendships have been formed on these tours by passengers who were previously strangers to each other. We also know that international travel is one of the best means of education that can be adopted, and we are every year confirmed in this view by the great number of sermons that are preached, lectures delivered, and books published by professional ladies and gentlemen in America and Europe.

The programmes we issue are compiled and placed before the public as the result of many years' *personal traveling experience*, based upon what ourselves and our responsible assistants know can be satisfactorily carried out within the time and cost specified. We set forth clearly and distinctly the routes of travel provided for, the time spent at each place, the hotels at which the party stops, defining exactly what the amount charged entitles the passenger to, besides giving a large amount of general information.

We never entrust our parties to the inexperienced guidance of men who have never been over the routes before, *nor to other contractors*, but we depend solely upon our own salaried staff to carry out the arrangements under our supervision. The conductors who travel with our parties are the recognized representatives of the firm, and are all gentlemen of education and experience, conversant with the languages and customs of the different countries, and who mingle with their parties on terms of perfect equality. Their office is to act as business manager, to engage accommodation at hotels, see to the arrangements for railway carriages, look after the baggage, and to relieve the passengers generally of the thousand and one annoyances that travelers in Europe are subjected to.

For ladies traveling without escort these parties will be found of great utility, advantage and protection, as they are always composed of refined and intelligent people.

We prepare all our programmes and itineraries for personally conducted parties with a full knowledge of our responsibility, and fully recognizing the fact that every one intrusting themselves to our care, does so in the hope that from the time they leave for Europe until they return, they may have their overworked and exhausted energies so relieved, and all the senses of pleasure and enjoyment so occupied, that they may derive all the benefit possible from the free and unfettered intercourse and commingling with foreign nationalities and scenes, and that they may return to their homes with expanded minds, enlarged and ennobled ideas, and renewed constitutions, strengthened to bear the duties before them.

Therefore, all who intrust themselves to our care may do so with the assurance that we know well that it is absolutely necessary that all travelers must return home satisfied that they have received value for the money expended, to insure the reputation of our firm being maintained.

For the coming season of 1881, we have arranged for

Three Grand Excursion Parties to Europe

AS FOLLOWS:

THE ANNUAL MAY PARTY

will leave New York by Steamship **BOTHNIA** of the **Cunard Line,** on Wednesday, **April 27th.** and full particulars are given on pages 11 to 20 of this pamphlet.

THE JUNE PARTY.

In order to meet the requirements of many ladies and gentlemen who desire to avail themselves of one of our parties, and who prefer going in the month of June, we have decided to advertise this special party to leave New York by Steamship **CITY OF RICHMOND** of the **Inman Line**, on Saturday, **June 11th.** Full particulars will be found on pages 21 to 32 of this pamphlet.

THE ANNUAL VACATION PARTY.

As usual, this party will be divided into three sections, and is organized for the convenience of the great number of travelers professionally engaged, students and others, who can only leave home during the Summer Vacation. The party will leave New York by one of the large Steamers of the **Anchor Line**, in all probability the *new* Steamship **FURNESSIA**, on Saturday, **July 2d.**

For full particulars as to this party see pages 33 to 50 of this pamphlet.

SPECIAL PARTY IN AUGUST.

Should there be a sufficient number of inquiries to justify it, we are prepared to make arrangements for a special party, to leave in August, to be in London the first week in September, at which time the **Ecumenical Methodist Conference** will meet. In this connection we may state that we shall be glad to supply tickets to delegates to the above Conference by any line of steamers they may select, at *reduced rates.*

In order to show in a more comprehensive form the routes over which these parties will travel, this pamphlet contains a specially engraved **Map of Europe**, which shows our extensive system of tours generally, and shows also the routes followed by our American Excursion parties.

A short description of the principal places of interest visited by our parties is also given on pages 55 to 61.

We invite all persons contemplating joining either of these parties to carefully study our programmes, and apply to our Chief American Office, 261 Broadway, New York, or any authorized Agency, if any further information or explanation is required.

In addition to the above brief intimations with reference to our parties, we also take pleasure in impressing upon intending American travelers the fact, that

Cook's International Traveling Tickets enable one or more Passengers to travel by all Chief Lines of Steamers and Railways to any part of, or Around the Globe, at any time, and do not compel the holders to travel in Parties.

Our system is so universal and comprehensive that we can meet the requirements of every class of travelers to any part of the globe they may wish to visit.

Intending travelers have only to send to our Chief American Office, 261 Broadway, New York, or any authorized Agency, an outline sketch of the tour they wish to take, stating the line of steamers, the route they wish to travel by, and the time to be occupied, and we will, in return, give them a correct quotation for the total fare for their proposed journeys.

Cook's Excursionist, American Edition, is published monthly in New York, and contains dates of sailing and fares by Transatlantic Lines of Steamers, and thousands of specimen tours to every part of the world, tickets for which are issued by us.

The EXCURSIONIST will be sent free by mail on receipt of 10 cents.

For the special comfort and convenience of those who do not wish to join a publicly advertised party, and, at the same time, wish to travel through Europe as comfortably as possible, and relieve themselves of the worry and anxiety of traveling alone and making their own arrangements, attending to their own baggage, securing hotel accommodation, etc., we are prepared to give quotations for

PRIVATE AND FAMILY PARTIES,

for whom, under special contract, we will undertake to send a qualified conductor for any tour they may select. Of course, the charge for such parties will be slightly higher, in proportion per passenger, than those made for the publicly advertised parties. All we require is, that at least three weeks' notice be given to our New York Office of the exact date the party will arrive in England, so that the necessary arrangements may be made for a competent conductor to meet them on landing from the steamer.

Passengers traveling in the ordinary way with our INTERNATIONAL TRAVELING TICKETS, will receive the free assistance of our salaried staff of representatives, who will be found at our various offices in all the chief cities in Europe and the East. They will be met on landing at the steamers, and assisted in Custom House examinations, etc.

THE HOTEL COUPON SYSTEM

has become a very large and important feature of our business, and secures to the holder good accommodation at over 500 first-class Hotels in various parts of the globe at a uniform rate of charge, and prevents the possibility of mistakes or overcharges. As these coupons were originated chiefly for the purpose of protecting our travelers, we do not, under any circumstances, issue the Hotel Coupons to any except those who travel under our arrangements, although we do issue traveling tickets without Hotel Coupons.

CIRCULAR NOTES AND LETTERS OF CREDIT.

Circular Notes, which are similar to Bank Drafts, are issued by us for the accommodation of tourists, and can be purchased at our Chief American Office, 261 Broadway, New York, and at our Chief Office, Ludgate Circus, London.

These Notes are of the value of £5 or £10 each, they are made payable to the order of the tourist, and must be endorsed by him when presented for payment. They are cashed at our Offices, at the AMERICAN EXCHANGE IN EUROPE, 449 Strand, London, W. C., at all of the Hotels on our list, by the Conductors of our parties, and by all recognized Bankers on the Continent and in the East. They have all the protection and conveniences of ordinary Circular Notes, and the special arrangements by which they are cashed at the Hotels obviate the delays which frequently arise to travelers who arrive at certain points after banking hours, and who would leave early the next morning but for the fact that they must lose a day, or a portion of a day, waiting for the opening of the Bank.

The Notes are accompanied by a Letter of Indication, showing a Statement of Account, and the list of places at which the Notes may be cashed. The Letter is signed by the tourist before leaving America,

COOK'S EUROPEAN EXCURSIONS. 9

and his signature serves to identify him. The Letter must always be shown when the Notes are presented for payment, but at all other times it should be carried *separately* from the Notes, so that in case the Notes are lost the finder will be unable to obtain payment.

These Notes are cashed at the current rate of exchange, and in the currency of the country where presented, and all Notes not used will be redeemed at the Chief American Office.

These Circular Notes have been issued in such large numbers during the past few years, that we felt justified, in 1878, in making

FOREIGN BANKING AND EXCHANGE

a special department of our business at our Chief Office in London, where travelers can exchange their Circular Notes obtained in America, and buy or sell current coin of the different countries of Europe.

In closing these introductory notes, we wish it to be distinctly understood that the system of

"COOK'S TOURS" IS THE EXCLUSIVE PROPERTY OF THOS. COOK & SON,

and that no individual, or firm, or agent, except those duly appointed and advertised by THOS. COOK & SON, have the right to use the title or system of the founders and sole proprietors,

THOS. COOK & SON.

CHIEF AMERICAN OFFICE,
261 BROADWAY, NEW YORK,
February 1st, 1881.

USEFUL HINTS FOR TOURISTS, CONCERNING EUROPEAN TRAVEL.

Passports.—As a rule, passports are unnecessary for the countries these parties will visit; still, if war should break out, passports might be needed. It only requires three days to get them from the State Department, and we will procure them for 50 cents each, in addition to the Government fee of $5. Applicants must fill up a blank, and swear to it before a notary, whose seal must be attached. The proper way to get them is to send us 50 cents for the blank, fill the blank up, have it properly attested by a notary, and return it to us with $5 enclosed. There are two kinds of blanks—one for native born, and the other for naturalized citizens. Naturalized citizens must send their naturalization papers with their application, and the papers will be returned with the passport.

Baggage.—It is of the greatest importance that passengers should take as little baggage with them on their tour as possible, as high rates are charged for extra baggage, especially on the Continent, and the limited weight allowed to tourists is 100 pounds on ocean steamers and up to London, 60 pounds being the weight allowed on the Continent of Europe. A strong medium-sized wooden or leather trunk is preferable, and where friends are traveling together, or in the case of married couples, a single trunk may serve for two persons. A small hand-bag or satchel, together with a shawl-strap, will be found of great convenience. Travelers should avoid overloading themselves with unnecessary bundles and packages. A most valuable and useful article is a small field or large opera-glass, which should have a strap attached, by which it can be carried over the shoulder.

A strong umbrella is frequently useful as a protection against sun and rain.

SPECIAL NOTE TO BE OBSERVED ABOUT BAGGAGE.

When leaving any hotel immediately after breakfast, to make a journey to another city, the trunks and small hand-bags should be packed, locked and strapped before leaving the bed-room. While at breakfast, the porters will remove all baggage, placing the small articles where you can lay your hands on them before entering the omnibus, and convey the large baggage to the station.

Labels for large baggage and hand baggage for the use of the members of our parties will be furnished by us upon application.

Clothing.—For the ocean passage, the tourist should provide himself for all kinds of weather. The clothing should be ample, to guard against chills, and outside wraps, hoods, shawls, overcoats, worsted leggins and rugs will be found highly useful. Ladies will find camel-hair serge or woolen dresses the best. Jewelry of value should not be taken, with the exception, perhaps, of one set, to be worn constantly. Gentlemen will find warm clothing throughout, with an overcoat, very serviceable, so that prolonged sojourns may be made upon the deck, and cold winds may be encountered without discomfort. All clothing worn on steamers may be left behind either at Glasgow, Liverpool, or at the American Exchange in Europe, 449 Strand, London, W. C., where it will be stored at a slight expense. For traveling on the Continent, ladies should have a traveling and walking dress, and a black silk or stylish costume for receptions or dress occasions. For gentlemen, a traveling suit, also a black suit for dress occasions. If a full-dress suit is found necessary, it may be hired at a slight expense at almost every place.

Washing.—In hotels on the Continent of Europe there are ample facilities for getting washing for travelers done quickly. It should be given to the chambermaid early in the day, and a list made out of the articles, with the day and hour at which they are required to be returned clearly written at the foot.

Washing books, in different languages, may be obtained at any of Cook's Tourist Offices.

Sundries.—A few suggestions as to some further requisites may be appreciated. A pocket compass will be found invaluable; a light scrap-book, and of a size easily disposed of in packing; a package or two of address or visiting cards; toilet soap; case with needles, thread, ball of string, buttons, scissors, penknife, and such other little articles as may suggest themselves and which may prove useful.

Medicines.—It is not our vocation to prescribe, but aperient or astringent medicines may be required, and quinine is not unfrequently of use. Parties would do well to consult their usual medical attendant on this subject before leaving. First-class physicians and apothecaries can be found in all principal cities in Europe, and usually in our parties there is some member of the medical profession. A little court plaster, extract of ginger, ammonia, arnica, or some kind of liniment, enter into every tourist's outfit.

Foreign Moneys.—On pages 8 and 9 of this pamphlet will be found an explanation of our Circular Notes and Letters of Credit and of our Foreign Banking and Exchange Department; and on 3d page of cover we also give a money table showing the relative value of European currencies.

Custom House Examinations.—All baggage is examined by the Custom House authorities in the various countries visited by these parties, and every assistance will be rendered by our conductors to facilitate this matter. Travelers should be in readiness with their keys and answer correctly, stating the contents of any trunks or parcels, and give to the officials every aid in the performance of their duty.

Languages.—Whilst a knowledge of some of the Continental languages is very useful, still persons traveling with our parties do not absolutely need to speak them, as the conductor acts as interpreter where necessary, and English is spoken by almost all of the hotel keepers, waiters and merchants throughout the Continent.

The traveler will do well to provide himself with a copy of the "Tourist's Conversational Guide to France, Germany and Italy," by J. T. Loth, which can be obtained at any of our offices, price 35 cents.

Guide Books and Maps.—A list of our Guide Books is shown on 2d page of cover.

ANNUAL MAY PARTY.

PROGRAMME OF
COOK'S
Special Personally Conducted Party
—TO—

ENGLAND, FRANCE, ITALY, SWITZERLAND, GERMANY,

The Rhine, Belgium and Holland,

VISITING

LONDON, PARIS, TURIN, GENOA, PISA, FLORENCE,

ROME. NAPLES. POMPEII,

Capri, Sorrento, Venice, Milan, Lake of Como, Lake Maggiore, the Simplon Pass, Chamounix, Geneva, Berne, Interlacken, Lucerne, Zurich, Schaffhausen, the Falls of the Rhine, Strasbourg, Baden-Baden, Heidelberg, Wiesbaden, the Rhine, Cologne, Brussels, Antwerp, Amsterdam, the Hague, Rotterdam, etc.

Leaving NEW YORK, WEDNESDAY, APRIL 27, 1881,
By Cunard Mail Steamer "BOTHNIA."

96 DAYS' TOUR, $600.

UNDER THE MANAGEMENT OF

THOS. COOK & SON,

Originators of the World-renowned Tourist and Excursion System (Established 1841), and only successful Conductors of Tours and Excursions to all parts of the Globe. Specially appointed by his Royal Highness the Prince of Wales, Sole Passenger Agents to the Royal British Commission, Vienna, 1873, Philadelphia, 1876, and Paris, 1878.

CHIEF OFFICE, LUDGATE CIRCUS, LONDON.
CHIEF AMERICAN OFFICE,
261 Broadway, New York.

INTRODUCTION.

We take pleasure in announcing our first personally conducted tour to Europe for the season of 1881. Favorable arrangements have been made by us with the CUNARD STEAMSHIP Co., whereby we are enabled to offer to applicants for this party a good selection of berths. The party will sail from New York on Wednesday, April 27th, by the S. S. "BOTHNIA," 4,500 tons burden, and one of the finest steamers of the Cunard fleet, Captain Murphy, Commander.

The programme for this party is based on the experience of past years, and, as will be seen, it includes the choicest and most interesting routes of European travel.

As this party will be limited in number, persons contemplating joining it should make early application to

THOMAS COOK & SON.

ITINERARY.

Wednesday, April 27th.—Leave New York by Steamship "BOTHNIA," from pier foot of Clarkson street, North River, at 3 p. m., for Liverpool.

N. B.— We are notified by the Steamship Company that the above-named Steamer is appointed to sail on this date; but we cannot, of course, hold ourselves responsible should any change be made and another Steamer substituted. This, however, is not likely to occur.

Sunday, May 8th.—Expect to arrive at **LIVERPOOL.** (*Washington Hotel.*)

Monday, May 9th.—Proceed to London by Midland Railway, going through the celebrated Derbyshire Peak district, and passing Chatsworth, Haddon Hall, Matlock Bath, Derby, Leicester, Bedford, etc. (*Midland Grand Hotel.*)

Members of this party wishing to proceed to London *via* Chester, Birmingham, Warwick, for Stratford-on-Avon and Oxford, will be supplied with tickets by Great Western Railway. The Conductor will travel *via* Midland Railway.

Tuesday, May 10th.
Wednesday, May 11th.
Thursday, May 12th.
Friday, May 13th.
Saturday, May 14th.
Sunday, May 15th.

IN LONDON. Owing to the great number of places of interest in the Metropolis, and the diversity of opinion as to which places should be visited, no formal programme for sight-seeing will be prepared, but every assistance and information will be afforded to the members of the party by our staff.

Monday, May 16th.—Leave London for Paris, *via* New Haven and Dieppe, by 8 p. m. train, from London Bridge Station.

Passengers who may so desire can take an afternoon train and spend a few hours at Brighton, joining the party at New Haven in the evening.

Any passenger preferring the short sea mail route, via Dover and Calais, can be supplied with tickets for that route on payment of the difference of fare.

Tuesday, May 17th.—Arrive in Paris. (*Hotel to be arranged.*)

Baggage examined at Paris on arrival.

Wednesday, May 18th.
Thursday, May 19th.
Friday, May 20th.
Saturday, May 21st.
Sunday, May 22d.

IN PARIS, three days of which will be devoted to carriage drives, visiting the principal places of interest in and around the city, including an excursion to St. Cloud, Sévres and Versailles, in accordance with the following programme :

FIRST DAY.

New French Opera, Grand Boulevards, La Madelaine, Place de la Concorde and Obelisk of Luxor, Champs Elysées, Palace of Industry, Palace of the Elysée, Arc de Triomphe de l'Etoile, Ecole Militaire, Invalides and Tomb of Napoleon, Ministry of Foreign Affairs, Palace Bourbon, Pont de la Concorde, Palace of the Legion of Honor, Palace of the Council of State (ruins), Tuileries, Palais Royal.

Bibliothèque Nationale, Bourse, Rue Lafayette, Square Montholon, St. Vincent de Paul, Northern Railway Terminus, Park of the Buttes Chaumont, Cemetery of Père la Chaise, Prison de la Roquette and Place of Execution, Place de la Bastille and Column of July, Place du Château d'Eau, Porte St. Martin, Porte St. Denis, La Trinité.

SECOND DAY.

St. Augustin, Park Monceau, Arc de Triomphe, Bois de Boulogne, the Lakes, Grand Cascade and Race-course, view of the Citadel of Mont Valérien, Town and Park of St. Cloud, Montretout-Buzenval, Forest of Ville d'Avray, Avenue de Picardie, Versailles, the Grand Trianon and State Carriages.

PALACE, MUSEUM AND PARK OF VERSAILLES, Avenue de Paris, Viroflay, Chaville, Sèvres and its Porcelain Manufactory (exterior), Billancourt, Fortifications of Paris, Viaduct of Anteuil, Palace of the Trocadéro, Seine Embankment, Cours la Reine.

THIRD DAY.

Column Vendôme, Garden of the Tuileries, Institute of France, Mint, Pont Neuf and Statue of Henry IV., Palace of Justice, Ste. Chapelle, Tribunal of Commerce, Conciergerie, Cour de Cassation, St. Germain l'Auxerrois, Palace and Museum of the Louvre, Palais Royal.

Place du Carrousel and Triumphal Arch, École des Beaux Arts, St. Germain des Prés, St. Sulpice, Palace of the Luxembourg, St. Jacques du Haut Pas, Val de Grâce, Carpet Manufactory of the Gobelins, Observatory, Statue of Marshal Ney, Fountain and Gardens of the Luxembourg, Panthéon, Bibliothèque Ste. Genevieve, St. Etienne du Mont, Fontaine Cuvier, Jardin des Plantes, Orléans Railway Terminus, Halle aux Vins, Morgue, Cathedral of Notre Dame, Hôtel Dieu, Place du Châtelet, the new Avenue de l'Opéra.

Monday, May 23d.—Leave Paris by 8 p. m. train for Turin, via Dijon, Macon and the Mount Cenis Tunnel.

Baggage examined either at Modane or Turin.

Tuesday, May 24th.—Arrive in Turin at 6 p. m. (*Hotel d'Angleterre.*)

Wednesday, May 25th.—IN TURIN, visiting the Royal Palace, Museums, Cathedral, squares, etc., and leaving by afternoon train for Genoa. (*Hotel de la Ville.*)

Thursday, May 26th.—IN GENOA, visiting the Cathedral, Church of the Annunziata, Palace of the Doges, Public Gardens, etc.

Friday, May 27th.—Leave Genoa by Riviera Railway for PISA. (*Hotel de Londres.*)

Saturday, May 28th.—The morning will be spent in viewing the Cathedral, Baptistry, Leaning Tower, Campo Santo, etc., leaving by noon train for Rome. (*Continental Hotel.*)

Sunday, May 29th. } IN ROME, three days of which will be devoted to
Monday, May 30th. } carriage excursions, under the superintendence of
Tuesday, May 31st. } Mr. Shakspere Wood, the eminent archæologist,
Wednesday, June 1st. } according to the following programme:

N. B. Special attention is called to the fact that, under an agreement between MR. SHAKSPERE WOOD and ourselves, our parties are the ONLY ones that do the sight-seeing of Rome under his charge.

FIRST DAY.

THE PALATINE.—The Seven Hills: remains of the Walls of Romulus and Port Mugonia: remains of Temples and edifices of the early Republic; remains of houses of the Republican period; House of Tiberius Claudius Nero, with Fresco paintings.

THE PALACE OF THE CÆSARS.—Site of the House of Augustus; Palace of Tiberius; substructions of the Palace of Caligula, and Porticos built by him to the Domus Tiberiana; great suite of State rooms, built by Domitian; Lararium, Basilica, Triclinium, etc.; Intermontium: great Stadium of Domitian; gigantic Porticos of Septimius Severus; site of Septizonium, etc., etc.

BASILICA OF CONSTANTINE.

ARCH OF TITUS.—Bas-relief of Soldiers carrying Seven-branched Candlestick, etc.

(AFTER LUNCH.)

THE COLOSSEUM.	TEMPLE OF VESTA.
TEMPLE OF VENUS AND ROME.	TEMPLE OF FORTUNA VIRILIS.
REMAINS OF DOMUS TRANSITORIA OF NERO.	PONTE ROTTO and View along the Tiber.
	THE CLOACA MAXIMA.
ARCH OF CONSTANTINE.	THEATRE OF MARCELLUS.
META SUDANS.	THE PORTICO OF OCTAVIA.

SECOND DAY.

THE PANTHEON.

THE FORUM ROMANUM.—Via Sacra ; Vicus Tuscus ; Clivus Capitulinus ; Temples of Castor and Pollux, the Deified Julius, Saturn, Vespasian, Concord , the Basilica Julia ; Honorary Monuments, the Pedestal of Domitian's Statue, Column of Phocas ; Rostrum ; Arch of Septimius Severus ; Portico of the Dei Consentes ; the Tabularium.

THE TARPEIAN ROCK.

THE MAMERTINE PRISON.

THE FORA OF THE EMPERORS Augustus, Nero, Trajan.

(AFTER LUNCH.)

THE GOLDEN HOUSE OF NERO.

BATHS OF TITUS.

BASILICA OF ST. CLEMENT : the Basilica of the Twelfth Century ; the now subterranean Basilica of the Fourth Century ; marvelously preserved Frescoes ; House of Clement : Temple of Mithras ; remains of a grand edifice of the Republican period, superimposed on a portion of the wall of the Kings, beneath the subterranean Basilica.

BASILICA OF ST. JOHN LATERAN.

THE SCALA SANCTA.

AQUEDUCT OF NERO.

BASILICA OF ST. PAUL, Outside the Walls.

THIRD DAY.

VATICAN MUSEUM OF SCULPTURE.

THE SIXTINE CHAPEL.—Michael Angelo's "Last Judgment."

STANZE AND LOGGIE OF RAPHAEL.

VATICAN PICTURE GALLERY.—"The Transfiguration ;" "Communion of St. Jerome ;" "Madonna di Foligno," etc., etc.

(AFTER LUNCH.)

BATHS OF CARACALLA ;   PORTA ST. SEBASTIANO ;   COLOMBARIA.

THE APPIAN WAY.—Tombs of Geta, Priscilla, Cecilia Metella, Seneca, the Cotta Family, &c., &c. ; Tumuli of the Horatii and Curiatii ; the Villa of the Quintilii; the Ustrinum; the Circus of Romulus: the Catacombs. (*See "New Guide to Ancient and Modern Rome," price* $2.00.)

During the stay in Rome a pleasant Excursion can be made by Steam Tramway to TIVOLI. Excursion tickets may be had at Cook's Tourist Office, 1 B Piazza di Spagna; price, $1.

Thursday, June 2d.—Leave by afternoon train for Naples. (*Grand Hotel Nobile.*)

Friday, June 3d.   IN NAPLES, during which time the party will visit the principal places of interest in the city and surroundings, including carriage drives to Herculaneum, Pompeii and Vesuvius, and a steamboat excursion on the Bay of Naples to the Island of Capri, visiting the Blue Grotto, weather permitting.
Saturday, June 4th.
Sunday, June 5th.
Monday, June 6th.

Tuesday, June 7th.—Go by morning train to Rome, sleeping at Rome. (*Continental Hotel.*)

Wednesday, June 8th.—Leave by morning train for Florence, *via* Torontola and Chiusi. (*Hotel d'Europe.*)

Thursday, June 9th.   IN FLORENCE, during which time visits will be made to the Tombs of the Medicis, the Cathedral and Baptistry, Church of Santa Croce (the Westminster Abbey of Italy), the Uffizi Gallery, Palaces of the Signoria and Pitti, etc.
Friday, June 10th.

Saturday, June 11th.—Leave Florence by morning train for Venice, *via* Bologna. The Railway line between Florence and Bologna, which intersects the Tuscan Apennines, is one of the grandest in Europe. Bridges, tunnels (45 in all), and galleries are traversed in uninterrupted succession. Beautiful views are obtained of the valleys and gorges of the Apennines and of the luxuriant plains of Tuscany, "the Garden of Italy." (*Hotel Victoria.*)

Sunday, June 12th.
Monday, June 13th.
Tuesday, June 14th.

IN VENICE, during which time gondolas will be provided for visiting the most important points of interest, including the Church of St. Marc, Royal Palace, the Palace of the Doges, the Bridge of Sighs, State Prisons, the principal Churches, Museums, Art Galleries, the Islands of the Lagoons, the Lido, etc.

Wednesday, June 15th.—Leave Venice for Milan, *via* Verona, Desenzano, Brescia, etc. Between Peschiera and Desenzano a view of the picturesque Lake of Garda is obtained. (*Grand Hotel de Milan.*)

Thursday. June 16th.
Friday, June 17th.

IN MILAN. Visiting the Cathedral dedicated to Marie Nascenti, one of the finest specimens of Gothic architecture in the world. The Gallery Vittorio Emanuele or Public Arcade, which is one of the most spacious and attractive of its kind in existence. The Arch of Peace, the Brera Collection of Pictures and Statues, the Church of Santa Maria delle Grazie, containing, in the Monastery, the celebrated "Last Supper" of Leonardo da Vinci, etc.
A National Exhibition, and a Musical Exhibition, will be open in Milan at this time, affording an opportunity for such members of the party as desire to visit them.
During the stay at Milan an excursion by rail and steamer will be made to the romantic LAKE OF COMO, visiting Bellagio and its charming surrounding villa.

Saturday, June 18th.—Leave by noon train for ARONA, thence by steamer on Lake Maggiore to Stresa, beautifully situated upon its shores, opposite the Borromean Islands. (*Hotel des Isles Borromees.*)

Sunday, June 19th.—A day of rest at STRESA.

Monday, June 20th.—Leave by diligence at 1 a. m., traveling through the magnificent and historic SIMPLON PASS, arriving at Brieg at 4.10 p. m. (*Hotel des Couronnes et Poste.*)

Tuesday, June 21st.—Leave Brieg by Simplon Railway for MARTIGNY. (*Hotel Clerc.*)

Wednesday, June 22d.—Go by mules or carriages over the TETE NOIR, to Chamounix. (*Hotel d'Angleterre.*)

Thursday, June 23d.
Friday, June 24th.

IN THE VALLEY OF CHAMOUNIX. The hotel here commands a magnificent view of MONT BLANC. Excursions may be made to the Montanvert, Mauvais Pas, Mer de Glace, Chapeau, Jardin, Flegere, or to the beautiful gorges of LA DIOZA.

Saturday, June 25th.—Leave by diligence through Sallanches, for Geneva. (*Hotel de Russie.*) Visits may be made to the Cathedral, where Calvin preached; the Russian Church, Rathhaus, Rousseau's Island, the meeting of the waters, etc.

Sunday, June 26th.—A day of rest IN GENEVA, situated on the banks of the romantic Lake Leman.

Monday, June 27th.—Leave Geneva by morning train for BERNE, stopping over a train at Fribourg (if considered advisable by the Conductor). (*Hotel Bellevue.*) A magnificent panorama of the snowy peaks of the Bernese Alps may be seen from the garden of the Hotel, or from the terrace of the Cathedral, on a fine day. The Cathedral (1421-1573) contains a celebrated organ, on which evening recitals are given. The Clock Tower, Bear Pit, Kindli-fresser, Gothic Church, Rathhaus, etc., constitute the sight-seeing of the Capital of Switzerland.

Tuesday, June 28th.—Leave Berne by morning express train for **INTER-LACKEN,** one of the most beautiful spots in Switzerland, and in full view of the Jungfrau. (*Hotel Victoria.*)

Wednesday, June 29th.—Carriages will be provided for an excursion to **GRIN-DELWALD,** to see the wonderful Glaciers. Short and pleasant walks may be made to Heimwehfluh, Unspunnen, Beatenberg, Thurnberg, etc., most of which places afford good views of the Lakes of Thun and Brienz.

Thursday, June 30th.—Go by afternoon boat to **GIESSBACH,** spending the night there and witnessing the illumination of the celebrated Falls. (*Giessbach Hotel.*)

Friday, July 1st.—By steamer to Brienz and by carriage over the picturesque **BRUNIG PASS** to Alpnacht, passing through Lungern and Sarnen, and by the Lake of that name (4½ miles long), taking steamer at Alpnacht, on the Lake of the Four Cantons, to Lucerne. (*Swan Hotel.*)

Saturday, July 2d. } **IN LUCERNE,** during which time an Excursion on
Sunday, July 3d. } the Lake and the ascent of the Righi will be made.

At Lucerne may be visited the Lion cut in solid rock, after design by Thorwaldsen, in memory of the Swiss Guards who fell in defending Louis XVI. against the revolutionary mob in Paris, Aug. 10th, 1792. The Glacier Garden, in which are many relics of lacustrine habitations, etc., adjoins the "Lion." The Cathedral, containing one of the best organs in Switzerland, and the quaint Church-yard, are full of interest. Old Bridges and Fortifications. The Lake of Lucerne (*Vierwaldstaedtersee*) is full of wild and picturesque scenery, and is associated with the legend of William Tell.

Monday, July 4th.—Go by convenient train, *via* Zug, to **ZURICH.** (*Hotel Bellevue.*) This town is noted for its manufactures. Places of interest are the Hohe Promenade, offering fine views, the Cathedral, Botanical Gardens, etc.

Tuesday, July 5th.—Go by morning train to Schaffhausen; thence by train or omnibus to **NEUHAUSEN** to see the **FALLS OF THE RHINE.** (*Hotel Schweizerhoff.*)

Wednesday, July 6th.—Leave by train over the Black Forest Railway, one of the greatest engineering achievements in Europe, passing Donaueschingen, (the source of the Danube), Triberg, Hornberg, Offenburg, etc. for **STRASBOURG.** (*Hotel Maison Rouge.*)

Thursday, July 7th.—Inspect the celebrated Cathedral and its wonderful clock, and thence proceed by train, *via* Kehl and Appenweier, to **BADEN-BADEN.** (*Hotel Hollande.*) A pleasant carriage excursion may be made from here into the Black Forest at a small cost.

Friday, July 8th.—Leave by train for **HEIDELBERG,** (*Hotel d'Europe,*) one of the charming spots in Rhenish Germany. Visit the Schloss and the Great Tun, the University, Cathedral, etc.

Saturday, July 9th.—Travel by train, *via* Darmstadt, to Frankfort, stopping here for a few hours, thence to Wiesbaden. (*Grand Hotel du Rhin.*)

Sunday, July 10th.—A day of rest **IN WIESBADEN.**

Monday, July 11th.—The party will be conveyed by carriages or omnibuses to **BIEBRICH,** where they will take steamer for the voyage down the Rhine to Cologne. The voyage on one of the magnificent saloon steamers, up or down the Rhine, is one of unsurpassed interest. The banks of this noble River teem with relics of by-gone feudal splendor—ruined castles, whose associations and whose legends awaken every generous feeling, as they glide by on either hand. The beauty and interest of the scenery are concentrated between Bingen and Bonn, for in quick succession we pass Eltville, Ruedesheim and Bingen, the Maus Thurm, Rheinstein, Lorch, Bacharach, Gutenfels, Schoenberg, the Lurlei, Rheinfelz, Boppart, Coblentz, with the Ehrenbreitstein, Andernach, Rheineck, Remagen, Godesburg, the Drachenfels, Seven Mountains, reaching Cologne early in the evening.—(*Hotel Disch.*)

Tuesday, July 12th.—**IN COLOGNE.** The morning may be spent in visiting the Cathedral, one of the finest Gothic churches in the world, begun in 1248; it was left unfinished from the beginning of the 16th century until 1816, and finally completed in August, 1880; church of St. Ursula (12th century), with the bones of 11,000 martyred virgins; Rathhaus (13th to 16th centuries).

Leave Cologne by express train, *ria* Aix la Chapelle, Verviers and Liege, for Brussels. (*Hotel de la Poste*.) *Baggage examined at Verviers.*

Wednesday, July 13th.	To be spent **IN BRUSSELS,** during which time the following places will be visited : The Hotel de la Ville, Wiertz Museum, the Palace of the Duke of
Thursday, July 14th.	Arenburg, Cathedral of St. Gudule, the House of Parliament ; also, carriage or railway excursion to the Battle-field of Waterloo.

Friday, July 15th.—Leave Brussels, *via* Malines, for **ANTWERP.** (*Hotel d'Europe*.) The remainder of the day may be spent in visiting the Cathedral, containing celebrated paintings by Rubens, the church of St. Jacques, the church of St. Paul, the Hotel de Ville, Museum, Zoological Gardens, etc., etc.

Saturday, July 16th.—Leave by morning train for **THE HAGUE.** (*Hotel Vieux Doelen*.) *Baggage examined at Roosendaal.* This is admitted to be the prettiest place in Holland. It is the seat of the Government, and contains the Museum, with the unrivalled collections of paintings, etc., including the renowned "Bull," by Paul Potter: the "School of Anatomy," by Rembrandt, etc. A visit to **SCHEVENINGEN,** the fashionable sea-side resort of the Dutch, is strongly recommended.

Sunday, July 17th.—A day of rest at **THE HAGUE.**

Monday, July 18th.—Leave by convenient train for Amsterdam. (*Old Bible Hotel*.)

Tuesday, July 19th.—**IN AMSTERDAM** visiting the Palace, Museum, Harbor and Docks, Diamond Factories, etc.

Wednesday, July 20th.—Proceed by morning train to **ROTTERDAM,** (*New Bath Hotel*) and visit the Groote Kerk (Church of St. Lawrence), Boyman's Museum, the Birthplace and Statue of Erasmus, and quaint streets. Leave same evening by Harwich steamer for London. *Baggage examined at Harwich.*

Thursday, July 21st.	(**IN LONDON.** (*Midland Grand Hotel*.)
Friday, July 22d.	} Leaving by evening express train on Friday for **LIV-ERPOOL.**

Saturday, July 23d.—Leave Liverpool by Cunard Line Steamer for New York.

Wednesday, Aug. 3d.—Expect to arrive at **NEW YORK.**

THE PRICE FOR THIS TOUR IS $600,

WHICH INCLUDES

First-class Ocean passage both ways,	20 Days.
First-class Hotel accommodation in Great Britain,	11 Days.
First-class Hotel accommodation on the Continent,	65 Days.

Total, 96 Days.

IT ALSO INCLUDES :

First-class railway and steamboat traveling for the entire journey; Omnibuses and Porterage between Stations and Hotels ; free transportation of 60 lbs. of Baggage; gratuities to Servants; three days' carriage drives in Paris; three days' carriages in Rome, and the services of Mr. Shakspere Wood; Trip to Pompeii and Vesuvius; Steamboat trip to Capri; two days' gondolas in Venice;. excursion from Milan to Lake Como and back; Carriages to Grindelwald; Excursion on Lake Lucerne and ascent of the Righi; Excursion to Waterloo; fees for sight-seeing, as per Conductor's Programme; services of special local guides where necessary; and also the services of the Conductor, who acts as Interpreter and Manager.

NOTE.—*The Conductor will only pay for carriages ordered by himself, and the services of the guides will be for the whole party.*

Hotel provision for each country to be according to the custom of the country, viz.: in Great Britain, Meat Breakfast, Table d'Hôte Dinner, Tea, Bedroom, lights, service and attendance. On the Continent: Meat Breakfast, Dinner at Table d'Hôte (with or without wine, as the Hotel provides), Bedroom, lights and service.

SPECIAL NOTICE.—Each person joining this party will also receive an admission ticket to the AMERICAN EXCHANGE IN EUROPE, free of charge, entitling the holder to all the privileges of the Exchange while the party is in London. For particulars see page 64.

STEAMSHIP ACCOMMODATION.

The Staterooms provided for this party are the best outside rooms. Three passengers will be placed in each room. Married couples will be assigned an entire inside room.

Married couples desiring large outside rooms can be accommodated on payment of $36 additional.

A DEPOSIT OF FIFTY DOLLARS

is required from each person who decides to go with this party; when the deposit is made, the name is registered, and the berths are allotted in the exact order of these deposits, the earliest depositors, of course, receiving the best berths.

Forty dollars of this deposit may be withdrawn up to April 10th, after which time the whole amount is due.

HOW TO JOIN THE PARTY.

Persons desirous of joining this party should write as early as possible, enclosing draft on any bank or postal order made payable to the order of THOS. COOK & SON. We will, upon receipt of the same, return a "Deposit Receipt" and a plan of the steamer, showing the location of the berths we can offer. Should the choice of berths be left to us, we will use our best judgment in the interest of each, and advise them at once. The balance of the money can be paid any time after April 10th.

SIZE OF THE PARTY.

In order to insure comfort, and secure good accommodation at Hotels, the number of passengers will be limited.

EXTENSION OF TIME.

BREAKS IN THE JOURNEY can be made at almost any point, and as the return steamship tickets are good for one year, any of the members of this party can remain in Europe at their discretion. The whole amount of fare must be paid before starting, but they can receive back the value of their unused tickets and Hotel coupons, less 10 per cent. (*Swiss Traveling Tickets excepted*), at the Chief London Office, or they can be exchanged for tickets to other points, at their full value.

On the return from the Continent, if any wish to extend their tour to the English Lakes, Scotland and Ireland, taking the steamer at Liverpool or Queenstown, quotations will be given by Messrs. THOS. COOK & SON; and if a party of 10 or more is made up for such supplementary tour, a Conductor will be sent with them, without extra charge.

A very interesting tour from London, combining the English Lakes, Melrose, Abbotsford, Edinburgh, Stirling, the Trossachs, Loch Lomond, Loch Katrine, Glasgow, Belfast, the Giant's Causeway, Dublin, and the Lakes of Killarney, thence to Queenstown to join the steamer, may be accomplished comfortably in from 10 to 12 days.

HOMEWARD ATLANTIC VOYAGE.

We have proved from experience that a large percentage of the passengers booked for Personally Conducted Parties do not return by the Atlantic steamers on the exact dates given in these itineraries, therefore we must impress upon the members of this party the importance of giving us the earliest possible notice and the date they intend leaving for New York, so that good berths may be secured for them.

Passengers failing to do this will have to take their own risk as to the location of berths that may be allotted them, when they finally give instructions for their return passage to be secured.

OTHER LINES OF STEAMERS.

Any who desire to avail themselves of this Tour, but prefer some other line of steamers, we can accommodate them, and will give them a special quotation either higher or lower, according to the line preferred. We will also, for those who have engaged steamship passage, give quotations, and book them from Liverpool, London or Paris.

DETOURS.

Any member will be allowed to leave the party to visit other localities, provided early notice be given to the Conductor, so that engagements for hotel accommodation may not be violated. Hotel coupons will be supplied to those who so leave the party for the number of days they expect to be absent. Any unused coupons to be redeemed at the advertised rate. No allowance can, however, be made for incidental expenses when not traveling with the Conductor.

BAGGAGE.

Whilst anxious to render all possible assistance to travelers in the transport, care and registration of baggage, THOS. COOK & SON cannot admit responsibility in cases of detention, stray conveyance, damage to or loss of baggage. In all cases of transference it is necessary that baggage should be identified by its owners, especially on entering and leaving hotels and railway stations ; and whenever baggage is subject to customs examination, its owners should be present to answer for it.

Great care will be taken in the registration and conveyance of the trunks or portmanteaus of the parties whilst traveling with the Conductor ; but it must be distinctly understood that all small packages, such as hand-bags, umbrellas, traveling rugs, &c., must remain entirely under the control of the passenger.

LABELS for large baggage and hand baggage for the use of the members of this party will be furnished by us upon application.

LETTERS may be addressed to any member of the party, care of THOMAS COOK & SON, LUDGATE CIRCUS, LONDON, and such letters will be carefully forwarded to the Conductor of the party for delivery.

LETTERS OF CREDIT AND CIRCULAR CHECKS are issued by us at current rates, in the denomination of five or ten pounds sterling each, and are payable at nearly every point on the route, or will be cashed by the Conductor as required, in the currency of the country where the party happens to be at the time.

They are also cashed at the AMERICAN EXCHANGE IN EUROPE, No. 449 Strand, London, W. C.

CAUTIONARY PROVISO.

The liability of Alpine roads and railroads in the neighborhood of mountains to damage from storms and other influences beyond human control, renders it necessary that we should announce that we cannot be responsible for detention or expenses incurred by deviation of routes occasioned by circumstances of this nature, nor for delays or deviations that may be caused through the railways being required for military purposes.

The most that Companies will do under such circumstances is to repay the value of any tickets or proportion of tickets not used for lines thus rendered impassable; and all claims in such cases must be sent in writing, accompanied by the unused tickets, within one month from the date for which such tickets were available.

THOS. COOK & SON,

P. O. Box 4197.   261 Broadway, New York.

COOK'S JUNE PARTY.

✳ PROGRAMME ✳

—OF A—

Special Personally Conducted Party,

LEAVING

NEW YORK on SATURDAY, JUNE 11th, 1881,

By Steamship "CITY OF RICHMOND," of the Inman Line,

INCLUDING VISITS TO THE MOST INTERESTING CITIES OF

Ireland, Scotland, England, Belgium, The Rhine District,

GERMANY, SWITZERLAND AND FRANCE,

WITH AN EXTENSION TOUR TO ITALY,

AND EMBRACING:

Cork, Blarney Castle, Glengariff, The Lakes of Killarney, Muckross Abbey, Dublin, Enniskillen,
Londonderry, The Giants' Causeway, Belfast, Glasgow, Loch Lomond, Loch Katrine,
The Trossachs, Stirling Castle, Edinburgh, Melrose Abbey, Abbotsford,

LONDON, ROTTERDAM, THE HAGUE, AMSTERDAM, ANTWERP,

Brussels, Cologne, The Rhine, Wiesbaden, Frankfort, Heidelberg, Schaffhausen, Zurich,
Lucerne, The Righi, The Bernese Oberland, Geissbach, Interlacken, The Jungfrau,
Grindelwald, Berne, Lausanne, Lake Leman, Bouveret, Martigny, The
Tete Noir Pass, Chamounix, Mt. Blanc, Geneva, Dijon, Paris,
Rouen, Dieppe, Brighton, London, The Derby-
shire Peak District, Liverpool, &c.

78 DAYS' TOUR, $500.

THE ITALIAN EXTENSION

Will include, in addition to the above, visits to TURIN, MILAN, VENICE, FLORENCE,
NAPLES, POMPEII, ROME, PISA AND GENOA,

Occupying 16 Days' Additional Time, at an Extra Cost of $125.

UNDER THE MANAGEMENT OF

THOS. COOK & SON,

Originators of the World-renowned Tourist and Excursion System (Established 1841), and only
successful Conductors of Tours and Excursions to all parts of the Globe. Specially
appointed by his Royal Highness the Prince of Wales, Sole Passenger
Agents to the Royal British Commission, Vienna 1873,
Philadelphia 1876, and Paris 1878.

CHIEF OFFICE, LUDGATE CIRCUS, LONDON.

CHIEF AMERICAN OFFICE,

261 Broadway, New York.

INTRODUCTION.

In order to meet the requirements of many ladies and gentlemen who desire to avail themselves of one of our parties, and who prefer going in the month of June, we have decided to advertise this special party to leave New York on Saturday, June 11th, by Steamship CITY OF RICHMOND of the INMAN LINE, 4,607 tons burden, Captain R. Leitch, Commander.

We have no doubt that this Tour, which embraces the most interesting parts of Ireland, Scotland, England and the Continent of Europe, will be appreciated by the traveling public, and persons contemplating joining this party should make early application, as the number of berths reserved is limited.

THOS. COOK & SON.

ITINERARY.

Saturday, June 11th.—Leave New York by Inman Line Steamship "CITY OF RICHMOND," from Pier foot of Charlton Street, at 3 p. m.

N. B.— We are notified by the Steamship Company that the above-named Steamer is appointed to sail on this date; but we cannot, of course, hold ourselves responsible should any change be made and another Steamer substituted. This, however, is not likely to occur.

Monday, June 20th.—Expect to land at **QUEENSTOWN,** (*Baggage examined on arrival*) and proceed to **CORK.** (*Imperial Hotel.*) If the passengers land early enough, they will be conducted to **BLARNEY CASTLE,** and have an opportunity of kissing the celebrated Blarney Stone on the day of their arrival. Should the passengers not land early enough, it will have to be omitted from the programme.

Tuesday, June 21st.—Leave Cork by railway *via* Bandon for Drimoleague, thence take jaunting cars, *via* Bantry Bay, to **GLENGARIFF,** resting the night at Glengariff. (*Roche's Hotel.*)

Wednesday, June 22d.—On the jaunting cars, *via* Kenmare, to Killarney. (*Railway Hotel.*)

Thursday, June 23d, Friday, June 24th. } . { To be spent **AT KILLARNEY.** Excursions will be arranged by boat and car to the interesting points of the lakes and district, including the Gap of Dunloe, Dinis, Ross and the other chief islands, Muckross Abbey, the Torc, and other waterfalls, etc., etc. During the stay the ascent of Mangerton can be made, which, if the weather is favorable, commands one of the finest panoramic views in Great Britain, and is well worth the little labor and fatigue required to make the ascent.

Saturday, June 25th.—Proceed by express train, *via* Mallow, to Dublin, arriving there the same evening. (*Imperial Hotel.*)

Sunday, June 26th.—To be spent **IN DUBLIN.**

Monday, June 27th.—Proceed by train, *via* Drogheda, Dundalk and Enniskillen, to **LONDONDERRY.** (*Jury's Hotel.*) Near Enniskillen the railway skirts a portion of the beautiful Loch Erne, and should the party consist of a sufficient number to justify it, the conductor will be in a position to arrange for a special steamboat trip over the Loch, in which case the party will not arrive at Londonderry until late at night.

Tuesday, June 28th.—The morning will be devoted to visiting the points of interest in Londonderry, leaving in the afternoon by train for PORTRUSH. If the weather is favorable and the evening fine, a jaunting car excursion will be made the same evening to the GIANTS' CAUSEWAY, where guides will be in attendance to point out all features of interest, and the peculiar formation of the Causeway and the neighboring caves. En route between Portrush and the Causeway, a view will be obtained of the ruins of the celebrated CASTLE OF DUNLUCE.

Wednesday, June 29th.—Leave Portrush by railway for Belfast. BELFAST is a well-known manufacturing and commercial city, but it does not contain any features of special interest to tourists, therefore we do not propose spending more than a few hours here, during which time the principal streets and points of interest can be visited, the party leaving the same night by the mail steamer for Glasgow, arriving early on the morning of

Thursday, June 30th.—GLASGOW, like Belfast, has very few features of interest to general tourists. The party will therefore visit the city during the early part of the day, and will proceed by afternoon train to BALLOCH, there to take the steamer on LOCH LOMOND to INVERSNAID.

Friday, July 1st.—Leave Inversnaid by coach for STRONOCHLACHER, there to take the steamer on LOCH KATRINE. At the head of Loch Katrine coaches are again taken, passing through the TROSSACHS district, skirting Lochs Achray and Venochar, passing over the historical Brig o' Turk to Callander, and thence by railway to STIRLING, where opportunity will be given for visiting the historical castle, from which views are obtained of the battle-field of Bannockburn, etc. Proceeding by railway the same night to Edinburgh. (*Philp's Cockburn Hotel.*)

Saturday, July 2d.
Sunday, July 3d.

IN EDINBURGH. Saturday will be devoted to the chief points of interest, including Calton Hill and Holyrood Palace, passing from thence through the old parts of the city, in which are to be seen the houses that were occupied by the former Kings and Nobles of Scotland, the house from which John Knox addressed the inhabitants of Edinburgh, etc., etc., to the castle. The chief rooms of the Castle will be visited, and all points of interest indicated by the guides, and the passengers will return from the Castle by the Public Gardens, Princess street, to the hotel.

Monday, July 4th.—Leave by early train, *via* the North British Railway, for MELROSE. Carriages will be taken for a visit to the ruined Abbey, and for a five mile drive to ABBOTSFORD, the home of Sir Walter Scott; then back to Melrose Station, when train will be taken for Carlisle; thence by Midland Railway through Leeds, Sheffield, Leicester, Bedford to London. (*Midland Grand Hotel.*)

Tuesday, July 5th.
Wednesday, July 6th.
Thursday, July 7th.
Friday, July 8th.

IN LONDON. Owing to the great number of places of interest in the Metropolis, and the diversity of opinion as to which places should be visited, no formal programme for sightseeing will be prepared, but every assistance and information will be afforded to the members of the party by our staff.
The party will leave London on Friday evening by Harwich or Flushing route for Rotterdam.

Saturday, July 9th.—Arrive at **ROTTERDAM** early (*New Bath Hotel*), (*Baggage examined on arrival*), visit the principal places of interest, leaving the same afternoon for Amsterdam. (*Old Bible Hotel.*)

Sunday, July 10th.—**IN AMSTERDAM,** one of the most interesting cities in northern Europe.

Monday, July 11th.—Leave by morning train, stopping for a brief visit to **THE HAGUE,** and reaching Antwerp the same evening. *Baggage examined at Roosendaal.* (*Hotel de l'Europe.*)

Tuesday, July 12th.—Spend the morning **IN ANTWERP,** visiting the Cathedral (containing celebrated paintings by Rubens), the church of St. Jacques, the church of St. Paul, the Hotel de Ville, Museum, Zoological Gardens, etc., leaving by afternoon train for Brussels. (*Hotel de la Poste.*)

Wednesday July 13th.
Thursday, July 14th.
{ To be spent **IN BRUSSELS,** during which time the following places will be visited: The Hotel de la Ville, Wiertz Museum, the Palace of the Duke of Arenberg, the Cathedral St. Gudule, the House of Parliament, etc., etc.

Friday, July 15th.—Leave Brussels by morning express train, *via* Liege, Verviers and Aix la Chapelle for **COLOGNE,** arriving early enough to visit the Cathedral, one of the finest Gothic churches in the world, begun in 1248, was left unfinished from the beginning of the 16th century until 1816, and finally completed in August, 1880; church of St. Ursula (13th century), with the bones of 11.000 martyred virgins, etc. (*Hotel Hollande.*) *Baggage examined at Cologne on arrival.*

Saturday, July 16th.—By one of the magnificent saloon steamers up the Rhine to **BIEBRICH.** The trip up or down the Rhine is one of unsurpassed interest. The banks of this noble river teem with relics of by-gone feudal splendor; ruined castles, whose associations and whose legends awaken every generous feeling as they glide by on either hand. The beauty and interest of the Rhine scenery are concentrated between Bonn and Bingen, for in quick succession we pass the Seven Mountains, the Drachenfels, Godesberg, Rheineck, Coblentz, with the Ehrenbreitstein, Boppart, Schoenberg, Gutenfels, Rheinstein, the Maus Thurm, Bingen and Eltville. At Biebrich carriages or omnibuses will convey the party to Wiesbaden. (*Grand Hotel du Rhin.*)

Sunday, July 17th.—A day of rest **IN WIESBADEN,** one of the most famous and attractive watering places in Germany.

Monday, July 18th.—Proceed to Heidelberg, *via* **FRANKFORT,** stopping for a few hours at the latter place.

Tuesday, July 19th.—**IN HEIDELBERG,** one of the charming spots in Rhenish Germany; visit the Schloss and Great Tun, University, Cathedral, etc.

Wednesday, July 20th.—Go by early morning train *via* Black Forest Railway to Schaffhausen, thence by train or omnibus to **NEUHAUSEN,** to see the **FALLS OF THE RHINE.** (*Hotel Schweitzerhoff.*) *Baggage examined on arrival at Schaffhausen.*

Thursday, July 21st.—After visiting the Falls of the Rhine, leave by afternoon train for **ZURICH.** This town is noted for its manufactures. Of interest are the Hohe Promenade, offering fine views, the Cathedral, Botanical Gardens, etc. (*Hotel Bellevue.*)

Friday, July 22d.—By afternoon train *via* Zug to Lucerne. (*Swan Hotel.*)

COOK'S JUNE PARTY.

Saturday, July 23d.
Sunday, July 24th.
} **IN LUCERNE**, during which time an excursion on the Lake and the ascent of the Righi will be made.

At Lucerne may be visited the Lion cut in solid rock, after design by Thorwaldsen, in memory of the Swiss Guards who fell in defending Louis XVI. against the revolutionary mob in Paris, Aug. 10th, 1792. The Glacier Garden, in which are many relics of lacustrine habitations, etc., adjoins the "Lion." The Cathedral, containing one of the best organs in Switzerland, and the quaint church-yard, are full of interest. Old Bridges and Fortifications. The Lake of Lucerne (*Vierwaldstaedtersee*) is full of wild and picturesque scenery, and is associated with the legend of William Tell.

Monday, July 25th. —Leave Lucerne by steamer on the Lake of the Four Cantons for Alpnacht, there to take carriages over the picturesque **BRUNIG PASS,** spending the night at **GIESSBACH** to witness the illumination at the celebrated Falls. (*Giessbach Hotel.*)

Tuesday, July 26th.—By steamer on Lake Brienz to Interlacken, one of the most beautiful spots in Switzerland, and in full view of the Jungfrau. (*Hotel Ritschard.*)

Wednesday, July 27th.
Thursday, July 28th.
} **IN INTERLACKEN,** during which time carriages will be provided for an excursion to Grindelwald, to see the wonderful glaciers. Short and pleasant walks may be made to Heimwehfluh, Unspunnen, Beatenberg, Thurnberg, etc., most of which places afford good views of the Lakes of Thun and Brienz.

Friday, July 29th.—By boat on the Lake of Thun, and by train to **BERNE.** (*Hotel Bellevue.*) A magnificent panorama of the snowy peaks of the Bernese Alps may be seen from the garden of the Hotel, or from the terrace of the Cathedral, on a fine day. The Cathedral (1421–1573) contains a celebrated organ, on which evening recitals are given. The Clock Tower, Bear Pit, Kindli-fresser, Gothic Church, Rathaus, etc., constitute the sightseeing of the Capital of Switzerland.

Saturday, July 30th.—By train to Lausanne, stopping a few hours at Friburg to hear the celebrated organ, if practicable. Thence by omnibus to Ouchy. (*Hotel Beau Rivage.*)

Sunday, July 31st.—A day of rest **IN OUCHY,** on the beautiful Lake Leman.

Monday, August 1st.—By steamer across Lake Leman, passing the Castle of Chillon, to Bouveret, where train will be taken for **MARTIGNY.** (*Hotel Clerc.*)

Tuesday, August 2d.—By mules or carriages over the **TETE NOIR** to Chamounix. (*Hotel d' Angleterre.*)

Wednesday, August 3d.—**IN THE VALLEY OF CHAMOUNIX.** The hotel here commands a magnificent view of MONT BLANC. Excursions may be made to the Montauvert, Mauvais Pas, Mer de Glace, Chapeau, Jardin, Flegere, or to the beautiful gorges of LA DIOZA.

Thursday, August 4th.—Leave by diligence through Sallanches for Geneva. (*Hotel Metropole.*)

Friday, August 5th.—**IN GENEVA,** situated on the banks of the romantic Lake Leman. Visits may be made to the Cathedral where Calvin preached, the Russian Church, Rath Museum, Rousseau's Island, the meeting of the waters, etc., leaving by 3.15 p. m. express train for Paris.

Saturday, August 6th.—Arrive in Paris at 5.15 a. m. (*Hotel to be arranged.*) *Baggage examined at Paris on arrival.*

Sunday, August 7th.
Monday, August 8th.
Tuesday, August 9th.
Wednesday, August 10th.
Thursday, August 11th.

IN PARIS, three days of which will be devoted to carriage drives, visiting the principal places of interest in and around the city, including an excursion to St. Cloud, Sévres and Versailles, according to the following programme:

FIRST DAY.

New French Opera, Grand Boulevards, La Madeleine, Place de la Concorde and Obelisk of Luxor, Champs Elysées, Palace of Industry, Palace of the Elysée, Arc de Triomphe de l'Etoile, Ecole Militaire, Invalides and Tomb of Napoleon, Ministry of Foreign Affairs, Palace Bourbon, Pont de la Concorde, Palace of the Legion of Honor, Palace of the Council of State (ruins), Tuileries, Palais Royal.

Bibliothèque Nationale, Bourse, Rue Lafayette, Square Montholon, St. Vincent de Paul, Northern Railway Terminus, Park of the Buttes Chaumont, Cemetery of Père la Chaise, Prison de la Roquette and Place of Execution, Place de la Bastille and Column of July, Place du Chateau d'Eau, Porte St. Martin, Porte St. Denis, La Trinité.

SECOND DAY.

St. Augustin, Park Monceau, Arc de Triomphe, Bois de Boulogne, the Lakes, Grand Cascade and Race-course, view of the Citadel of Mont Valérien, Town and Park of St. Cloud, Montretout-Buzenval, Forest of Ville d'Avray, Avenue de Picardie, Versailles, the Grand Trianon and State Carriages.

PALACE, MUSEUM AND PARK OF VERSAILLES, Avenue de Paris, Viroflay, Chaville, Sèvres and its Porcelain Manufactory (exterior), Billancourt, Fortifications of Paris, Viaduct of Auteuil, Palace of the Trocadéro, Seine Embankment, Cours la Reine.

THIRD DAY.

Column Vendome, Garden of the Tuileries, Institute of France, Mint, Pont Neuf and Statue of Henry IV., Palace of Justice, Ste. Chapelle, Tribunal of Commerce, Conciergerie, Cour de Cassation, St. Germain l'Auxerrois, Palace and Museum of the Louvre, Palais Royal.

Place du Carrousel and Triumphal Arch, Ecole des Beaux Arts, St. Germain des Près, St. Sulpice, Palace of the Luxembourg, St. Jacques du Haut Pas, Val de Grace, Carpet Manufactory of the Gobelins, Observatory, Statue of Marshal Ney, Fountain and Gardens of the Luxembourg, Panthéon, Bibliothèque Ste. Génévieve, St. Etienne du Mont, Fontaine Cuvier, Jardin des Plantes, Orleans Railway Terminus, Halle aux Vins, Morgue, Cathedral of Notre Dame, Hôtel Dieu, Place du Chatelet, the new Avenue de l'Opéra.

Friday, August 12th.—Leave Paris by morning service for London, going through the beautiful Valley of the Seine, passing Rouen and Dieppe, taking steamer at this last place for Newhaven, reaching London same evening. (*Midland Grand Hotel.*) *Baggage examined at Newhaven.*

Any passenger preferring the short sea mail route, via Calais and Dover, can be supplied with tickets for that route on payment of the difference of fare.

Saturday, August 13th.
Sunday, August 14th.

IN LONDON.

Monday, August 15th.—Proceed by morning express train to LIVERPOOL, and spend the remainder of the day visiting the docks, Royal Exchange and other places of interest. (*Washington Hotel.*)

Tuesday, August 16th.—Sail from Liverpool by Inman Line steamer for Queenstown.

Wednesday, August 17th.—Arrive at QUEENSTOWN, take mails and sail for New York.

Saturday, August 27th.—Expect to arrive at NEW YORK.

THE PRICE FOR THIS TOUR IS $500,

WHICH INCLUDES

First-class Ocean passage both ways,	20 Days.
First-class Hotel accommodation in Great Britain,	23 Days.
First-class Hotel accommodation on the Continent,	35 Days.

Total, 78 Days.

IT ALSO INCLUDES

First-class railway and steamboat traveling for the entire journey; Omnibuses and Porterage between Stations and Hotels; free transportation of 60 lbs. of baggage; gratuities to servants; jaunting cars to Blarney Castle and the Giants' Causeway; also to the lower lake at Killarney, returning by boats through the gap of Dunloe; Carriages to Abbotsford; Carriage Excursion to Grindelwald; three days' carriage drives in Paris; fees for sight-seeing as per Conductor's programme ; services of special local guides where necessary, and also the services of the Conductor, who acts as Interpreter and manager.

NOTE— *The Conductor will only pay for carriages ordered by himself, and the services of the guides will be for the whole of the party.*

Hotel provision for each country to be according to the custom of the country, viz.: in Great Britain, Meat Breakfast, Table d'Hote Dinner, Tea, Bedroom, lights, services and attendance. On the Continent, Meat Breakfast, Dinner at table d'Hote (with or without wine as the Hotel provides), Bedroom, lights and service.

SPECIAL NOTICE.— Each person joining this party will also receive an admission ticket to the AMERICAN EXCHANGE IN EUROPE, free of charge, entitling the holder to all the privileges of the Exchange while the party is in London. For particulars see page 64.

THE ITALIAN EXTENSION.

Should there be ten or more passengers desirous to extend their tour to Italy, we will undertake to send a special conductor from Geneva to travel in accordance with the following

ITINERARY.

Friday, August 5th.—Leave Geneva by afternoon train for TURIN, (*Hotel Trombetta.*) *Baggage examined at Modane or Turin.*

Saturday, August 6th.—Spend the morning in TURIN, visiting the Royal Palace, Musuems, Cathedral, squares, etc., and leaving by afternoon train for Milan. (*Hotel d'Europe.*)

Sunday, August 7th.—A day of rest at MILAN.

The Cathedral, dedicated to Maria Nascenti, is one of the finest specimens of Gothic architecture in the world. The Gallery Vittorio Emanuele or Public Arcade, is the most spacious and attractive of its kind in existence. The Arch of Peace, the Brera Collection of Pictures and Statues, the Church of Santa Maria delle Grazie, containing in the Monastery the celebrated "Last Supper" of Leonardo da Vinci, etc.

Monday, August 8th.—Leave by noon express train for Venice, *via* Brescia, Verona, Padua, etc. Between Desenzano and Peschiera a fine view of the picturesque Lake of Garda is obtained. Reach Venice at 7.10 p. m. (*Hotel Victoria.*)

Tuesday, August 9th.
Wednesday, Aug. 10th { **IN VENICE,** during which time gondolas will be provided for visiting the most important points of interest, including the Church of St. Marc, Royal Palace, the Palace of the Doges, the Bridge of Sighs, State Prisons, the principal Churches, Museums, Art Galleries, the Islands of the Lagoons, the Lido, etc., etc.

Thursday, August 11th.—Leave by morning train, *via* Bologna, for Florence. (*Hotel New York.*) The Railway line between Bologna and Florence, which intersects the Tuscan Apennines, is one of the grandest in Europe. Bridges, tunnels, (45 in all), and galleries are traversed in uninterrupted succession. Beautiful views are obtained of the valleys and gorges of the Apennines and of the luxuriant plains of Tuscany, "the Garden of Italy."

Friday, August 12th.—**IN FLORENCE,** visiting the Tombs of the Medicis, the Cathedral and Baptistry, Church of Santa Croce (the Westminster Abbey of Italy), the Uffizi Gallery, Palaces of the Signoria and Pitti, etc., etc.

Saturday, August 13th.—By morning express train, *via* Torontola, Chiusi and Rome to **NAPLES.** (*Hotel Metropole.*)

Sunday, August 14th.
Monday, August 15th. { **IN NAPLES,** during which time the party will visit the principal places of interest in the city and surroundings, including carriage or railway trip to **POMPEII.**

Tuesday, August 16th.—By morning train to Rome. (*Hotel d'Allemagne.*)

Wednesday, August 17th.
Thursday, August 18th.
Friday, August 19th. { **IN ROME,** two days will be devoted to carriage excursions, under the superintendence of Mr. Shakspere Wood, the eminent archæologist, according to a programme to be specially prepared by him, leaving at 3 p. m. on Friday for Pisa. (*Hotel de Londres.*)

N. B.—*Special attention is called to the fact that, under an agreement between* Mr. Shakspere Wood *and ourselves, our parties are the* only *ones that do the sight-seeing of Rome under his charge.*

Saturday, August 20th.—The morning will be spent at **PISA** in viewing the Cathedral, Baptistry, Leaning Tower, Campo Santo, etc., leaving by noon train by the Riviera Railway for Genoa. (*Hotel de la Ville.*)

Sunday, August 21st.—**IN GENOA.** Of interest are the Cathedral, Church of the Annunziata, Palace of the Doges, Public Gardens, etc.

Monday, August 22d.—Leave by early morning International Express train for Paris. (*Hotel to be arranged.*) *Baggage examined on arrival in Paris.*

Tuesday, August 23d.
Wednesday, August 24th.
Thursday, August 25th.
Friday, August 26th. { **IN PARIS,** three days of which will be devoted to carriage drives, visiting the principal places of interest in and around the city, including an excursion to St. Cloud, Sevres and Versailles, in accordance with the programme of main party on page 27.

Saturday, August 27th.—Leave by day service, *via* Rouen, Dieppe and Newhaven, for London. (*Midland Grand Hotel.*) *Baggage examined at Newhaven.*

Any passenger preferring the short sea mail route, via Calais and Dover, can be supplied with tickets for that route on payment of the difference of fare.

Sunday, August 28th.—IN LONDON.

Monday, August 29th.—Proceed by morning express train to LIVERPOOL, and spend the remainder of the day visiting the Docks, Royal Exchange and other places of interest. (*Washington Hotel.*)

Tuesday, August 30th.—Sail from Liverpool by Inman Line steamer for Queenstown.

Wednesday, August 31st.—Arrive at QUEENSTOWN, take mails and sail for New York.

Saturday, September 10th.—Expect to arrive at NEW YORK.

THE ADDITIONAL PRICE FOR THE ITALIAN EXTENSION IS $125,

WHICH INCLUDES,

In addition to all that is mentioned in the conditions of the main party, 16 days' hotel accommodation in Italy, one day gondolas in Venice, carriage or rail excursion to Pompeii, two days' carriages in Rome, and the services of Mr. Shakspere Wood.

STEAMSHIP ACCOMMODATION.

The Staterooms provided for this party are the best outside rooms. Three passengers will be placed in each room. Married couples will be assigned an entire inside room.

Married couples desiring large outside rooms can be accommodated on payment of $36 additional.

For the return ocean voyage passengers are entitled to the same accommodation, viz., two passengers in an inside room, or three passengers in an outside room, in accordance with the regulations of the Steamship Co.

A DEPOSIT OF FIFTY DOLLARS

is required from each person who decides to go with this party; when the deposit is made, the name is registered, and the berths are allotted in the exact order of these deposits, the earliest depositors, of course, receiving the best berths.

Forty dollars of this deposit may be withdrawn up to May 25th, after which time the whole amount is due.

HOW TO JOIN THE PARTY.

Persons desirous of joining this party should write as early as possible, enclosing draft on any bank or postal order made payable to the order of THOS. COOK & SON. We will, upon receipt of the same, return a "Deposit Receipt" and a plan of the steamer, showing the location of the berths we can offer. Should the choice of berths be left to us, we will use our best judgment in the interest of each, and advise them at once. The balance of the money can be paid any time after May 25th.

SIZE OF THE PARTY.

In order to insure comfort and secure good accommodation at Hotels, the number of passengers will be limited.

EXTENSION OF TIME.

BREAKS IN THE JOURNEY can be made at almost any point, and as the return steamship tickets are good for one year, any of the members of this party can remain in Europe at their discretion. The whole amount of fare must be paid before starting, but they can receive back the value of their unused tickets and Hotel coupons, less 10 per cent. (*Swiss Traveling Tickets excepted*), at the Chief London Office, or they can be exchanged for tickets to other points, at their full value.

HOMEWARD ATLANTIC VOYAGE.

We have proved from experience that a large percentage of the passengers booked for Personally Conducted Parties do not return by the Atlantic steamers on the exact dates given in these itineraries, therefore we must impress upon the members of this party the importance of giving us the earliest possible notice and the date they intend leaving for New York, so that good berths may be secured for them.

Passengers failing to do this will have to take their own risk as to the location of berths that may be allotted them, when they finally give instructions for their return passage to be secured.

OTHER LINES OF STEAMERS.

Any who desire to avail themselves of this Tour, but prefer some other line of steamers, we can accommodate them, and will give them a special quotation either higher or lower, according to the line preferred. We will also, for those who have engaged steamship passage, give quotations, and book them from Liverpool, London or Paris.

DETOURS.

Any member will be allowed to leave the party to visit other localities, provided early notice be given to the Conductor, so that engagements for hotel accommodation may not be violated. Hotel coupons will be supplied to those who so leave the party for the number of days they expect to be absent. Any unused coupons to be redeemed at the advertised rate. No allowance can, however, be made for incidental expenses when not traveling with the Conductor.

BAGGAGE.

Whilst anxious to render all possible assistance to travelers in the transport, care and registration of baggage, THOS. COOK & SON cannot admit responsibility in cases of detention, stray conveyance, damage to or loss of baggage. In all cases of transference it is necessary that baggage should be identified by its owners, especially on entering and leaving hotels and railway stations; and whenever baggage is subject to customs examination, its owners should be present to answer for it.

Great care will be taken in the registration and conveyance of the trunks or portmanteaus of the parties whilst traveling with the Conductor; but it must be distinctly understood that all small packages, such as hand-bags, umbrellas, traveling rugs, &c., must remain entirely under the control of the passenger.

LABELS for large baggage and hand baggage for the use of the members of this party will be furnished by us upon application.

LETTERS may be addressed to any member of the party, care of THOMAS COOK & SON, LUDGATE CIRCUS, LONDON, and such letters will be carefully forwarded to the Conductor of the party for delivery.

LETTERS OF CREDIT AND CIRCULAR CHECKS are issued by us at current rates, in the denomination of five or ten pounds sterling each, and are payable at nearly every point on the route, or will be cashed by the Conductor as required, in the currency of the country where the party happens to be at the time.

They are also cashed at the AMERICAN EXCHANGE IN EUROPE, No. 449 Strand, London, W. C.

CAUTIONARY PROVISO.

The liability of Alpine roads and railroads in the neighborhood of mountains to damage from storms and other influences beyond human control, renders it necessary that we should announce that we cannot be responsible for detention or expenses incurred by deviation of routes occasioned by circumstances of this nature, nor for delays or deviations that may be caused through the railways being required for military purposes.

The most that Companies will do under such circumstances is to repay the value of any tickets or proportion of tickets not used for lines thus rendered impassable; and all claims in such cases must be sent in writing, accompanied by the unused tickets, within one month from the date for which such tickets were available.

THOS. COOK & SON,

P. O. Box 4197.   261 Broadway, New York.

COOK'S
ANNUAL VACATION PARTY TO EUROPE,

For 1881.

PROGRAMME AND ITINERARIES
FOR THREE SECTIONS,

Including Visits to the most interesting Cities of

Scotland, England, Belgium, Germany, Switzerland,
ITALY AND FRANCE,

AND INCLUDING ALSO

The River Rhine, Mountain Passes of Switzerland, the Glaciers, Mt. Blanc, the Italian Lakes, Pompeii, etc.

Section I. Providing for **60 Days' Tour, - $350.**
Section II.—   "   " **74**   "   "   - **450.**
Section III.—   "   " **88**   "   "   - **500.**

Designed and arranged for the convenience of persons professionally engaged, Students and others, who can only leave home during the Summer Vacation.

TO LEAVE NEW YORK

By one of the large Anchor Line Steamers, sailing on Saturday, July 2d, 1881.

UNDER THE MANAGEMENT OF

THOS. COOK & SON,

Originators of the World-renowned Tourist and Excursion System (Established 1841), and only successful Conductors of Tours and Excursions to all parts of the Globe. Specially appointed by his Royal Highness the Prince of Wales. Sole Passenger Agents to the Royal British Commission, Vienna, 1873, Philadelphia, 1876, and Paris, 1878.

CHIEF OFFICE, LUDGATE CIRCUS, LONDON.

CHIEF AMERICAN OFFICE,
261 Broadway, New York.

INTRODUCTION.

We have the pleasure of announcing that this party will be conveyed to Glasgow by one of the large ANCHOR LINE Steamers—in all probability the *new* steamship "FURNESSIA," sailing Saturday, July 2d; and that we have entered into special arrangements with the above Steamship Company, whereby we are enabled to offer a good selection of berths, and, with the exception of a few forward rooms (where three passengers will be placed), all the rooms in the after-part of the ship will be occupied by *two persons only*, thus rendering the ocean voyage as pleasant and comfortable as possible. Early application for berths should be made by persons contemplating joining either of the sections of this party.

The steamship "FURNESSIA," Capt. John J. Small, Commander, is the largest and finest steamer of the Anchor Line fleet, and is 5,500 tons burden. She was built at the Barrow shipbuilding yard, and was launched in October, 1880. The steamers of this line are specially adapted for conveying large parties comfortably, owing to their great size, comfort and safety; and are fitted up in a grand and luxurious style, being provided with a large dining saloon amidships, and elegant music-room with piano and cabinet organ. A large library containing standard works is to be found in the music saloon. The staterooms are provided with all modern improvements and are well lighted and ventilated, and the table and attendance are first-class.

With these remarks, the itineraries of the three sections constituting this party are respectfully submitted.

THOMAS COOK & SON.

THE FIRST SECTION PROVIDES

FOR VISITING

Scotland, England, Belgium, the Rhine District, Germany, Switzerland and France,

AND INCLUDES

GLASGOW, LOCH LOMOND, LOCH KATRINE, THE TROSSACHS,

Stirling Castle, Edinburgh, Melrose, Abbotsford, London, Antwerp, Brussels, Cologne, the Rhine, Mayence, Worms, Heidelberg, Bale, Lucerne,

THE ASCENT OF THE RIGHI, THE BERNESE OBERLAND,

Giessbach, Interlacken, Grindelwald, Berne, Lausanne, Lake Leman, Bouveret, Martigny, the Tete Noir, Chamounix,

MONT BLANC, GENEVA, PARIS, ROUEN, DIEPPE AND BRIGHTON.

60 DAYS' TOUR, $350.

Itinerary of the First Section.

Saturday, July 2d.—Leave New York, by Anchor Line steamer "FURNESSIA" from pier foot of Dey Street at 9 A. M., for Glasgow.

N. B.— We are notified by the Steamship Company that the above-named Steamer is appointed to sail on this date; but we cannot, of course, hold ourselves responsible should any change be made and another Steamer substituted. This, however, is not likely to occur.

Wednesday, July 13th.—Expect to reach **GLASGOW.** (*Cockburn Hotel.*) *Baggage examined on arrival.*

Thursday, July 14th.—Go by early morning train to Balloch, and take steamer on **LOCH LOMOND** for Inversnaid, passing Inch Cailliach, Inch Murrin, and Inch Lonaig. Thence by coaches to **STRONACHLACHER,** and by steamer on **LOCH KATRINE** to the Trossachs, past Rob Roy's cave and Ellen's Isle. Coaches will then be taken, passing Loch Achray and Coilantogle Ford to Callander, thence by rail to Stirling, visiting the Royal Castle, etc., and continuing the journey, passing the Field of Bannockburn and Linlithgow Castle to Edinburgh. (*Cockburn Hotel.*)

Friday, July 15th.—**IN EDINBURGH,** visiting Holyrood Palace and Chapel, Edinburgh Castle, the Scott Monument, Calton Hill and the other attractions of this interesting city.

Saturday, July 16th.—Leave by early train, *via* the North British Railway, for **MELROSE.** Carriages will be taken there for a visit to the ruined Abbey, and for a five-mile drive to **ABBOTSFORD,** the home of Sir Walter Scott; then back to Melrose Station, when train will be taken for Carlisle; thence by Midland Railway through Leeds, Sheffield, Leicester, and Bedford to London. (*Midland Grand Hotel.*)

Sunday, July 17th.
Monday, July 18th.
Tuesday, July 19th.
Wednesday, July 20th.

IN LONDON. Owing to the great number of places of interest in the Metropolis, and the diversity of opinion as to which places should be visited, no formal programme for sight-seeing will be prepared, but every assistance and information will be afforded to the members of the party by our staff. The party will leave London by Flushing or Harwich route at 8.35 p. m. on Wednesday, for Antwerp.

Thursday, July 21st.—Arrive at **ANTWERP** about 10 a. m. (*Hotel d' Europe.*) *Baggage examined on arrival.*

Visits will be made to the Cathedral, containing celebrated paintings by Rubens, the church of St. Jacques, the church of St. Paul, the Hotel de Ville, Museum, Zoological Gardens, etc., leaving by afternoon train for Brussels. (*Hotel de la Poste.*)

Friday, July 22d.—**IN BRUSSELS,** during which time the following places will be visited: the Hotel de la Ville, Wiertz Museum, the Palace of the Duke of Arenberg, the Cathedral of St. Gudule, the House of Parliament, etc.

Saturday, July 23d.—Leave Brussels by morning express train, *via* Aix la Chapelle, for **COLOGNE,** arriving early enough to visit the Cathedral and other points of interest ; the Cathedral is one of the finest Gothic churches in the world, begun in 1248, was left unfinished from the beginning of the 16th century until 1816, and finally completed in August, 1880; church of St. Ursula (12th century), with the bones of 11,000 martyred virgins ; Rathhaus (13th to 16th centuries). (*Hotel Disch.*) *Baggage examined on arrival at Cologne.*

Sunday, July 24th.—A day of rest at **COLOGNE.**

Monday, July 25th.—Leave Cologne by morning train for Bonn, thence by one of the magnificent saloon steamers for Bingen and **MAYENCE.** The voyage up the Rhine is one of unsurpassed interest. The banks of this noble river teem with relics of by-gone feudal splendor—ruined castles, whose associations and whose legends awaken everygenerous feeling, as they glide by on either hand. The beauty and interest of the Rhine scenery are concentrated between Bonn and Bingen, for in quick succession we pass the Seven Mountains, the Drachenfels, Godesberg, Remagen, Rheineck, Andernach, Coblentz, with the Ehrenbreitstein, Boppart, Rheinfelz, the Lurlei, Schonberg, Rheinstein, the Maus Thurm, etc. (*Hotel Hollande.*)

Tuesday, July 26th.—Go from Mayence, *via* Worms, to Heidelberg, stopping for a few hours at **WORMS** to see the famous monument to Luther and other Reformers. (*Hotel d' Europe.*)

Wednesday, July 27th.—**IN HEIDELBERG,** one of the charming spots in Rhenish Germany; visit the Schloss and Great Tun, the University, Cathedral, etc.

Thursday, July 28th.—Travel, *via* Offenburg and Freiburg, to **BALE.** (*Hotel Trois Rois.*)

Friday, July 29th.—Leave by noon train, *via* Olten, for Lucerne. (*Swan Hotel.*)

Saturday, July 30th.   **IN LUCERNE,** during which time an excursion on the
Sunday, July 31st.   lake and the ascent of the Righi will be made.

At Lucerne may be visited the Lion cut in solid rock, after designs by Thorwaldsen, in memory of the Swiss Guards who fell in defending Louis XVI. against the revolutionary mob in Paris, Aug. 10th, 1792. The Glacier Garden, in which are many relics of lacustrine habitations, &c., adjoins the "Lion." The Cathedral, containing one of the best organs in Switzerland, and the quaint Church-yard, are full of interest. Old Bridges and Fortifications. The Lake of

Lucerne (*Vierwaldstaedtersee*) is full of wild and picturesque scenery, and is associated with the legend of William Tell.

Monday, August 1st.—By steamer to Alpnacht, thence by carriage over the picturesque **BRUNIG PASS**, passing through Sarnen and Lungern, and spending the night at **GIESSBACH**, witnessing the illumination of the celebrated Falls. (*Giessbach Hotel.*)

Tuesday, August 2d.—By morning boat on the Lake of Brienz to **INTER-LACKEN**, one of the most beautiful spots in Switzerland, and in full view of the Jungfrau. (*Hotel Victoria.*) Carriages will be provided for the members of the party desiring to visit **GRINDELWALD.** Short and pleasant walks may be made to Heimwehfluh, Unspunnen, Beatenberg, Thurnberg, &c., most of which places afford good views of the Lakes of Thun and Brienz.

Wednesday, August 3d.—By boat on Lake Thun and railway to **BERNE.** (*Hotel Bellevue.*) A magnificent panorama of the snowy peaks of the Bernese Alps may be seen from the garden of the Hotel or from the terrace of the Cathedral, on a fine day. The Cathedral (1421-1573) contains a celebrated organ, on which evening recitals are given. The Clock Tower, Bear Pit, Kindli-fresser, Gothic Church, Rathhaus, &c., constitute the sight-seeing of the capital of Switzerland.

Thursday, August 4th.—By afternoon train to **LAUSANNE**, situated on the northern bank of the Lake of Geneva. The Cathedral is the grandest Gothic structure in Switzerland. Vevey, Clarens, Castle of Chillon, Villeneuve, Montreux, etc., on the eastern shore of the Lake, may be visited from Ouchy, which is the port of Lausanne. A railway worked by hydraulic power connects Lausanne with Ouchy. (*Hotel Gibbon.*)

Friday, August 5th.—By steamer across Lake Leman, passing the Castle of Chillon to Bouveret, where train will be taken for **MARTIGNY.** (*Hotel Clerc.*)

Saturday, August 6th.—Go by mules or carriages over the **TETE NOIR** to Chamounix. (*Hotel d'Angleterre.*)

Tuesday, August 9th.—Leave by diligence through Sallanches for **GENEVA.** (*Hotel du Lac.*) Visits may be made to the Cathedral where Calvin preached, the Russian Church, Rath's Museum, Rousseau's Island, the meeting of the waters, &c.

Wednesday, August 10th.—Leave by afternoon express train for Paris. (*Hotel to be arranged.*) *Baggage examined on arrival in Paris.*

Thursday, August 11th.	**IN PARIS**, three days of which will be devoted to carriage drives, visiting the principal places of interest in and around the city, including an excursion to St. Cloud, Sèvres and Versailles, in accordance with the following programme :
Friday, August 12th.	
Saturday, August 13th.	
Sunday, August 14th.	
Monday, August 15th.	

FIRST DAY.

New French Opera, Grand Boulevards, La Madelaine, Place de la Concorde and Obelisk of Luxor, Champs Elysées, Palace of Industry, Palace of the Elysée, Arc de Triomphe de l'Etoile, Ecole Militaire, Invalides and Tomb of Napoleon, Ministry of Foreign Affairs, Palace Bourbon, Pont de la Concorde, Palace of the Legion of Honor, Palace of the Council of State (ruins), Tuileries, Palais Royal.

Bibliothèque Nationale, Bourse, Rue Lafayette, Square Montholon, St. Vincent de Paul, Northern Railway Terminus, Park of the Buttes Chaumont, Cemetery of Père la Chase, Prison de la Roquette and Place of Execution, Place de la Bastille and Column of July, Place du Château d'Eau, Porte St. Martin, Porte St. Denis, La Trinité.

SECOND DAY.

St. Augustin, Park Monçeau, Arc de Triomphe, Bois de Boulogne, the Lakes, Grand Cascade and Race-course, view of the Citadel of Mont Valérien, Town and Park of St. Cloud, Montretout-Buzenval, Forest of Ville d'Avray, Avenue de Picardie, Versailles, the Grand Trianon and State Carriages.

PALACE, MUSEUM AND PARK OF VERSAILLES, Avenue de Paris, Viroflay, Chaville, Sèvres and its Porcelain Manufactory (exterior), Billancourt, Fortifications of Paris, Viaduct of Auteuil, Palace of the Trocadéro, Seine Embankment, Cours la Reine.

THIRD DAY.

Column Vendôme, Garden of the Tuileries, Institute of France, Mint, Pont Neuf and Statue of Henry IV., Palace of Justice, Ste. Chapelle, Tribunal of Commerce, Conciergerie, Cour de Cassation, St. Germain l'Auxerrois, Palace and Museum of the Louvre, Palais Royal.

Place du Carrousel and Triumphal Arch, Ecole des Beaux Arts, St. Germain des Prés, St. Sulpice, Palace of the Luxembourg, St. Jacques du Haut Pas, Val de Grace, Carpet Manufactory of the Gobelins, Observatory, Statue of Marshal Ney, Fountain and Gardens of the Luxembourg, Panthéon, Bibliothèque Ste. Genevieve, St. Etienne du Mont, Fontaine Cuvier, Jardin des Plantes, Orléans Railway Terminus, Halle aux Vins, Morgue, Cathedral of Notre Dame, Hôtel Dieu, Place du Châtelet, the new Avenue de l'Opéra.

Tuesday, August 16th.—Go by day service, via Rouen, Dieppe and Brighton, to London. (*Midland Grand Hotel.*) *Baggage examined at Newhaven.*

Any passenger preferring the short sea mail route, via Calais and Dover, can be supplied with tickets for that route on payment of the difference of fare.

Wednesday, August 17th.—IN LONDON, leaving by evening express train for Glasgow. (*Cockburn Hotel.*)

Thursday, August 18th.—Leave GLASGOW or Greenock by Anchor Line steamer for New York.

Sunday, August 28th.—Expect to arrive at NEW YORK.

THE PRICE FOR THE FIRST SECTION IS $350,

WHICH INCLUDES

First-class Ocean passage both ways,	22 Days.
First-class Hotel accommodation in Great Britain,	10 Days.
First-class Hotel accommodation on the Continent,	28 Days.
Total,	60 Days.

IT ALSO INCLUDES :

First-class railway and steamboat traveling for the entire journey; omnibuses and porterage between stations and hotels; free transportation of 60 lbs. of baggage; gratuities to servants; carriages to Abbotsford; excursion on Lake Lucerne and ascent of the Righi; carriage excursion to Grindelwald; three days' carriage drives in Paris ; fees for sight-seeing, as per Conductor's programme ; services of special local guides where necessary; and also the services of the Conductor, who acts as interpreter and manager.

NOTE.—*The Conductor will only pay for carriages ordered by himself, and the services of the Guides will be for the whole of the party.*

Hotel provision for each country to be according to the custom of the country, viz.: in Great Britain, meat breakfast, table d'hote dinner, tea, bedroom, lights, services and attendance. On the Continent, meat breakfast, dinner at table d'hote (with or without wine as the Hotel provides), bedroom, lights and service.

SPECIAL NOTICE.—Each person joining this party will also receive an admission ticket to the AMERICAN EXCHANGE IN EUROPE, free of charge, entitling the holder to all the privileges of the Exchange while the party is in London. For particulars see page 64.

THE SECOND SECTION PROVIDES

FOR VISITING

Scotland, England, Belgium, the Rhine District,

GERMANY, SWITZERLAND, ITALY AND FRANCE,

AND INCLUDES

*Glasgow, Loch Lomond, Loch Katrine, the Trossachs, Stirling Castle,
Edinburgh, Melrose, Abbotsford, London, Antwerp, Brussels,
Cologne, the Rhine, Mayence, Worms, Heidelberg,
Bale, Lucerne, the Ascent of the Righi,*

THE BERNESE OBERLAND, GIESSBACH, INTERLACKEN,

GRINDELWALD, BERNE, LAUSANNE, LAKE LEMAN, BOUVERET,

MARTIGNY, THE TETE NOIR, CHAMOUNIX, MONT BLANC,

*Geneva, the Mont Cenis Tunnel, Turin, Milan, Venice, Florence. Rome,
Pisa, Genoa. Paris, Rouen, Dieppe and Brighton.*

74 DAYS' TOUR, $450.

Itinerary of the Second Section.

Saturday, July 2d.—Leave New York, by Anchor Line steamer "FURNESSIA,"
from pier foot of Dey Street at 9 a. m., for Glasgow.

N. B.— We are notified by the Steamship Company that the above-named Steamer will probably sail on this date; but we cannot, of course, hold ourselves responsible should any change be made and another Steamer substituted.

Wednesday, July 13th.—Expect to reach **GLASGOW.** (*Cockburn Hotel.*) *Baggage examined on arrival.*

Thursday, July 14th.—Go by early morning train to Balloch, and take steamer
on **LOCH LOMOND** for Inversnaid, passing Inch Cailliach, Inch Murrin, and
Inch Lonaig. Thence by coaches to **STRONACHLACHER,** and by steamer on
LOCH KATRINE to the Trossachs, past Rob Roy's cave and Ellen's Isle.
Coaches will then be taken, passing Loch Achray and Coilantogle Ford to Callander, thence by rail to Stirling, visiting the Royal Castle, etc., and continuing
the journey, passing the Field of Bannockburn and Linlithgow Castle to Edinburgh. (*Cockburn Hotel.*)

Friday, July 15th.—**IN EDINBURGH,** visiting Holyrood Palace and Chapel,
Edinburgh Castle, the Scott Monument, Calton Hill and the other attractions of
this interesting city.

Saturday, July 16th.—Leave by early train, *via* the North British Railway, for
MELROSE. Carriages will be taken there for a visit to the ruined Abbey, and

for a five-mile drive to **ABBOTSFORD,** the home of Sir Walter Scott; then back to Melrose Station, where train will be taken for Carlisle; thence by Midland Railway, through Leeds, Sheffield, Leicester and Bedford, to London. (*Midland Grand Hotel.*)

Sunday, July 17th.
Monday, July 18th.
Tuesday, July 19th.
Wednesday, July 20th.

IN LONDON. Owing to the great number of places of interest in the Metropolis, and the diversity of opinion as to which places should be visited, no formal programme for sight-seeing will be prepared, but every assistance and information will be afforded to the members of the party by our staff. The party will leave London by Flushing or Harwich route at 8.35 p. m., on Wednesday, for Antwerp.

Thursday, July 21st. Arrive at **ANTWERP** about 10 a. m. (*Hotel d' Europe.*) *Baggage examined on arrival.*

Visits will be made to the Cathedral containing celebrated paintings by Rubens, the church of St. Jacques, the church of St. Paul, the Hotel de Ville, Museum, Zoological Gardens, etc., leaving by afternoon train for Brussels. (*Hotel de la Poste.*)

Friday, July 22d.—**IN BRUSSELS,** during which time the following places will be visited : the Hotel de la Ville, Wiertz Museum, the Palace of the Duke of Arenberg, the Cathedral of St. Gudule, the House of Parliament, etc.

Saturday, July 23d.- Leave Brussels by morning express train, *via* Aix la Chapelle, for **COLOGNE,** arriving early enough to visit the Cathedral and other points of interest; the Cathedral is one of the finest Gothic churches in the world, begun in 1248, was left unfinished from the beginning of the 16th century until 1816, and finally completed in August, 1880; Church of St. Ursula (12th century), with the bones of 11,000 martyred virgins; Rathhaus (13th to 16th centuries). (*Hotel Disch.*) *Baggage examined on arrival at Cologne.*

Sunday, July 24th.—A day of rest at **COLOGNE.**

Monday, July 25th.—Leave Cologne by morning train for Bonn, thence by one of the magnificent saloon steamers for Bingen and **MAYENCE.** The voyage up the Rhine is one of unsurpassed interest. The banks of this noble river teem with relics of by-gone feudal splendor—ruined castles, whose associations and whose legends awaken every generous feeling, as they glide by on either hand. The beauty and interest of the Rhine scenery are concentrated between Bonn and Bingen, for in quick succession we pass the Seven Mountains, the Drachenfels, Godesberg, Remagen, Rheineck, Andernach, Coblentz, with the Ehrenbreitstein, Boppart, Rheinfelz, the Lurlei, Schonberg, Rheinstein, and Maus Thurm, etc. (*Hotel Hollande.*)

Tuesday, July 26th.—Go from Mayence, *via* Worms, to Heidelberg, stopping for a few hours at **WORMS** to see the famous monument to Luther and other Reformers. (*Hotel d' Europe.*)

Wednesday, July 27th.—**IN HEIDELBERG,** one of the charming spots in Rhenish Germany; visit the Schloss and Great Tun, the University, Cathedral, etc.

Thursday, July 28th.—Travel, *via* Offenburg and Freiburg, to **BALE.** (*Hotel Trois Rois.*)

Friday, July 29th.—Leave by noon train, *via* Olten, for Lucerne. (*Swan Hotel.*)

Saturday, July 30th.
Sunday, July 31st.

IN LUCERNE, during which time an excursion on the lake and the ascent of the Righi will be made.

At Lucerne may be visited the Lion cut in solid rock, after designs by Thorwaldsen, in memory of the Swiss Guards who fell in defending Louis XVI. against the revolutionary mob in Paris, Aug. 10th, 1792. The Glacier Garden, in which are many relics of lacustrine habitations, etc., adjoins the "Lion." The Cathedral, containing one of the best organs in Switzerland, and the quaint church-yard, are full of interest. Old Bridges and Fortifications. The Lake of Lucerne (*Vierwaldstaedtersee*) is full of wild and picturesque scenery, and is associated with the legend of William Tell.

Monday, August 1st.—By steamer to Alpnacht, thence by carriage over the picturesque **BRUNIG PASS**, passing through Sarnen and Lungern, and spending the night at **GIESSBACH**, witnessing the illumination of the celebrated Falls. (*Giessbach Hotel.*)

Tuesday, August 2d.—By morning boat on the Lake of Brienz to **INTER-LACKEN**, one of the most beautiful spots in Switzerland, and in full view of the Jungfrau. (*Hotel Victoria.*) Carriages will be provided for the members of the party desiring to visit **GRINDELWALD**. Short and pleasant walks may be made to Heimwehflüh, Unspunnen, Beatenberg, Thurnberg, etc., most of which places afford good views of the Lakes of Thun and Brienz.

Wednesday, August 3d.—By boat on Lake Thun and railway to **BERNE**. (*Hotel Bellevue.*) A magnificent panorama of the snowy peaks of the Bernese Alps may be seen from the garden of the Hotel, or from the terrace of the Cathedral, on a fine day. The Cathedral (1421-1573) contains a celebrated organ, on which evening recitals are given. The Clock Tower, Bear Pit, Kindli-fresser, Gothic Church, Rathhaus, &c., constitute the sight-seeing of the capital of Switzerland.

Thursday, August 4th.—By afternoon train to **LAUSANNE**, situated on the northern bank of the Lake of Geneva. The Cathedral is the grandest Gothic structure in Switzerland. Vevey, Clarens, Castle of Chillon, Villeneuve, Montreux, etc., on the western shore of the Lake, may be visited from Ouchy, which is the port of Lausanne. A railway worked by hydraulic power connects Lausanne with Ouchy. (*Hotel Gibbon.*)

Friday, August 5th.—By steamer across Lake Leman, passing the Castle of Chillon to Bouveret, where train will be taken for **MARTIGNY**. (*Hotel Clerc.*)

Saturday, August 6th.—Go by mules or carriages over the **TETE NOIR** to Chamounix. (*Hotel d'Angleterre.*)

Sunday, August 7th.
Monday, August 8th. } **IN THE VALLEY OF CHAMOUNIX**. The hotel here commands a magnificent view of Mont Blanc: excursions may be made to the Montanvert, Mauvais Pas, Mer de Glace, Chapeau, Jardin, Flegere, or to the beautiful gorges of La Dioza.

Tuesday, August 9th.—Leave by diligence through Sallanches, for Geneva. (*Hotel du Lac.*)

Wednesday, August 10th.—**IN GENEVA**. Visits may be made to the Cathedral where Calvin preached, the Russian Church, Rath's Museum, Rousseau's Island, the Meeting of the Waters, etc.

Thursday, August 11th.—Leave Geneva by morning train for **TURIN**, arriving at 6.20 p. m. (*Hotel d'Angleterre.*) *Baggage examined at Modane or Turin.*

Friday, August 12th.—Morning train to **MILAN**. (*Grand Hotel de Milan.*) The principal sights of Milan are the cathedral, dedicated to Marie Nascenti, one of the finest specimens of Gothic architecture in the world ; the Gallery Vittorio Emanuele or Public Arcade, which is one of the most spacious and attractive of its kind in existence ; the Arch of Peace, the Brera Collection of Pictures and Statues, the Church of Santa Maria delle Grazie, containing, in the Monastery, the celebrated "Last Supper" of Leonardo da Vinci.

Saturday, August 13th.—Leave by noon express train for Venice, *via* Brescia, Verona, Padua, etc. Between Desenzano and Peschiera a fine view of the picturesque Lake of Garda is obtained. Reach Venice at 7.10 p. m. (*Hotel Victoria.*)

Sunday, August 14th.
Monday, August 15th. } **IN VENICE**, during which time gondolas will be provided for visiting the most important points of interest, including the Church of St. Marc, Royal Palace, the Palace of the Doges, the Bridge of Sighs, State Prisons, the principal Churches, Museums, Art Galleries, the Islands of the Lagoons, the Lido, etc., etc.

Tuesday, August 16th.—Leave by morning train, *via* Bologna, for Florence. The Railway line between Bologna and Florence, which intersects the Tuscan Apennines, is one of the grandest in Europe. Bridges, tunnels (45 in all), and galleries are traversed in uninterrupted succession. Beautiful views are obtained of the valleys and gorges of the Apennines and of the luxuriant plains of Tuscany, "the Garden of Italy." (*Hotel de Russie.*)

Wednesday, August 17th.—**IN FLORENCE,** visiting the Tombs of the Medicis, the Cathedral and Baptistry, Church of Santa Croce (the Westminster Abbey of Italy), the Uffizi Gallery, Palaces of the Signoria and Pitti, etc., etc.

Thursday, August 18th.—By morning express train, *via* Torontola and Chiusi, to Rome. (*Hotel Continental.*)

Friday, August 19th. } **IN ROME,** two days of which will be devoted to
Saturday, August 20th. } carriage excursions, under the superintendence of
Sunday, August 21st. } Mr. Shakspere Wood, the eminent archæologist, ac-
Monday, August 22d. } cording to a special programme to be arranged by
him. The party will leave by 3 p. m. train on
Monday for Pisa. (*Hotel de Londres.*)

N. B.—Special attention is called to the fact that, under an agreement between Mr. SHAKSPERE WOOD *and ourselves, our parties are the* ONLY *ones that do the sight-seeing of Rome under his charge.*

During the stay in Rome a pleasant Excursion can be made by Steam Tramway to TIVOLI. Excursion tickets may be had at Cook's Tourist Office, 1 B. Piazza di Spagna; price $1.

Tuesday, August 23d.—The morning will be spent in **PISA** viewing the Cathedral, Baptistry, Leaning Tower, Campo Santo, etc., leaving by noon train by the Riviera Railway for Genoa. (*Hotel de la Ville.*)

Wednesday, August 24th.—**IN GENOA,** visiting the Cathedral, Church of the Annunziata, Palace of the Doges, Public Gardens, etc.

Thursday, August 25th.—Leave by early morning International Express train for Paris. (*Hotel to be arranged.*) *Baggage examined on arrival in Paris.*

Friday, August 26th. } **IN PARIS.** Three days to be devoted to carriage
Saturday, August 27th. } drives, visiting the principal places of interest in
Sunday, August 28th. } and around the city, including an excursion to St.
Monday, August 29th. } Cloud, Sèvres and Versailles, according to the pro-
gramme shown in first section, pages 37 and 38.

Tuesday, August 30th.—Leave by night service, *via* Rouen. Dieppe and Brighton, for London. (*Midland Grand Hotel.*) *Baggage examined at New Devhan.*

Any passenger preferring the short sea mail route, via Calais and Dover, can be supplied with tickets for that route on payment of the difference of fare.

Wednesday, August 31st.—**IN LONDON.** Leaving by evening express train for Glasgow. (*Cockburn Hotel.*)

Thursday, September 1st.—Leave **GLASGOW** or Greenock by Anchor Line steamer for New York.

Sunday, September 11th.—Expect to arrive at **NEW YORK.**

THE PRICE FOR THE SECOND SECTION IS $450,

WHICH INCLUDES

First-class Ocean passage both ways,   22 Days.
First-class Hotel accommodation in Great Britain,   11 Days.
First-class Hotel accommodation on the Continent,   41 Days.

Total, 74 Days.

IT ALSO INCLUDES :

First-class-railway and steamboat traveling for the entire journey; omnibuses and porterage between stations and hotels; free transportation of 60 pounds of baggage; gratuities to servants; carriages to Abbotsford; excursion on Lake Lucerne, and ascent of the Righi; carriage excursion to Grindelwald; gondolas for one day in Venice; two days' carriages in Rome and the services of Mr. Shakspere Wood; three days' carriage drives in Paris; fees for sight-seeing, as per Conductor's programme; services of special local guides where necessary, and also the services of the Conductor, who acts as Interpreter and Manager.

NOTE.—*The Conductor will only pay for carriages ordered by himself, and the services of the guides will be for the whole party.*

Hotel provision for each country to be according to the custom of the country, viz.: in Great Britain, meat breakfast, table d'hote dinner, tea, bedroom. lights, service and attendance. On the Continent: meat breakfast, dinner at table d'hote (with or without wine, as the Hotel provides), bedroom, lights and service.

SPECIAL NOTICE.—Each person joining this party will also receive an admission ticket to the AMERICAN EXCHANGE IN EUROPE free of charge, entitling the holder to all the privileges of the Exchange while the party is in London. For particulars see page 64.

THE THIRD SECTION PROVIDES

FOR VISITING

Scotland, England, Belgium, the Rhine District,

GERMANY, AUSTRIA, ITALY, SWITZERLAND AND FRANCE,

AND INCLUDES

Glasgow, Loch Lomond, Loch Katrine, the Trossachs, Stirling Castle. Edinburgh, Melrose, Abbotsford, London, Antwerp, Brussels, Cologne, the Rhine, Mayence, Worms, Heidelberg, Stuttgart, Munich, Innsbruck, Verona, Venice,

FLORENCE, ROME, NAPLES, POMPEII, PISA, GENOA,

Turin, Milan, Lake Maggiore, the Simplon Pass, Martigny, the Tete Noir, Chamounix, Geneva, Berne, Interlacken, Grindelwald, the Bernese Oberland, Lucerne, the Righi,

BALE, PARIS, ROUEN, DIEPPE, BRIGHTON.

88 DAYS' TOUR, $500.

Itinerary of the Third Section.

Saturday, July 2d.—Leave New York by Anchor Line steamer "FURNESSIA," from Pier foot of Dey Street at 9 a. m., for Glasgow.

N. B.—We are notified by the Steamship Company that the above-named Steamer will probably sail on this date; but we cannot, of course, hold ourselves responsible should any change be made and another Steamer substituted.

Wednesday, July 13th.—Expect to reach **GLASGOW.** (*Cockburn Hotel.*) *Baggage examined on arrival.*

Thursday, July 14th.—Go by early morning train to Balloch, and take steamer on **LOCH LOMOND** for Inversnaid, passing Inch Cailliach, Inch Murrin, and

Inch Lonaig. Thence by coaches to **STRONACHLACHER**, and by steamer on **LOCH KATRINE** to the Trossachs, past Rob Roy's Cave and Ellen's Isle. Coaches will be then taken, passing Loch Achray and Coilantogle Ford to Callander; thence by rail to Stirling, visiting the Royal Castle, etc., and continuing the journey, passing the Field of Bannockburn and Linlithgow Castle to Edinburgh. (*Cockburn Hotel.*)

Friday, July 15th. **IN EDINBURGH,** visiting Holyrood Palace and Chapel, Edinburgh Castle, the Scott Monument, Calton Hill, and the other attractions of this interesting city.

Saturday, July 16th.—Leave by early train, *via* the North British Railway, to **MELROSE.** Carriages will be taken there for a visit to the ruined Abbey, and for a five-mile drive to **ABBOTSFORD,** the home of Sir Walter Scott; then back to Melrose Station, where train will be taken for Carlisle; thence by Midland Railway through Leeds, Sheffield, Leicester and Bedford to London. (*Midland Grand Hotel.*)

Sunday, July 17th.
Monday, July 18th.
Tuesday, July 19th.
Wednesday, July 20th.

IN LONDON. Owing to the great number of places of interest in the Metropolis, and the diversity of opinion as to which places should be visited, no formal programme for sight-seeing will be prepared, but every assistance and information will be afforded to the members of the party by our staff.

Thursday, July 21st. Leave London by Flushing route at 8.35 p. m. for Antwerp.

Friday, July 22d.—Arrive at **ANTWERP** about 10 a. m. (*Hotel d'Europe.*) *Baggage examined on arrival.*

Visits will be made to the Cathedral, containing celebrated paintings by Rubens, the Church of St. Jacques, the Church of St. Paul, the Hotel de Ville, Museum, Zoological Gardens, etc., leaving by afternoon train for Brussels. (*Hotel de la Poste.*)

Saturday, July 23d.—**IN BRUSSELS,** during which time the following places will be visited: The Hotel de la Ville, Wiertz Museum, the Palace of the Duke of Arenberg, the Cathedral of St. Gudule, the House of Parliament, etc.

Sunday, July 24th. A day of rest **IN BRUSSELS.**

Monday, July 25th.—Leave Brussels by morning express train, *via* Aix la Chapelle, for **COLOGNE,** arriving early enough to visit the Cathedral and other points of interest. The Cathedral is one of the finest Gothic churches in the world, begun in 1248, was left unfinished from the beginning of the 16th century until 1816, and finally completed in August, 1880; Church of St. Ursula (12th century), with the bones of 11,000 martyred virgins; Rathhaus (13th to 16th centuries). (*Hotel Hollande.*) *Baggage examined on arrival at Cologne.*

Tuesday, July 26th.—Leave Cologne by rail for Bonn, thence by one of the magnificent saloon steamers for Bingen and **MAYENCE.** The voyage up the Rhine is one of unsurpassed interest. The banks of this noble river teem with relics of by-gone feudal splendor -ruined castles, whose associations and whose legends awaken every generous feeling, as they glide by on either hand. The beauty and interest of the Rhine scenery are concentrated between Bonn and Bingen, for in quick succession we pass the Seven Mountains, the Drachenfels, Godesberg, Remagen, Rheineck, Andernach, Coblentz, with the Ehrenbreitstein, Boppart, Rheinfelz, the Lurlei, Schonberg, Rheinstein, the Maus Thurm. (*Hotel Hollande.*)

Wednesday, July 27th.—Go from Mayence, *via* Worms, to Heidelberg, stopping for a few hours at **WORMS** to see the famous monument to Luther and other Reformers. (*Hotel d'Europe.*)

Thursday, July 28th.—**IN HEIDELBERG,** one of the charming spots in Rhenish Germany; visit the Schloss and Great Tun, the University, Cathedral, etc.

Friday, July 29th.—Go from Heidelberg, *via* Bruchsal, Stuttgart and Ulm (stopping a few hours at Stuttgart, if desirable), to Munich. (*Hotel Bellevue.*)

Saturday, July 30th.
Sunday, July 31st.
{ **IN MUNICH,** visiting the old Cathedral (built in 1488), the Royal Palace, Royal Bronze Foundry, Art Gallery, etc.

Monday, August 1st.—Leave Munich by morning train, *via* Innsbruck, Botzen and Ala, crossing the **BRENNER PASS** (4485 ft.) for Verona. (*Hotel de Londres.*)

Tuesday, August 2d.—Spend the morning in **VERONA,** visiting the house and tomb of Juliet, Tombs of the Scaligeri, Arch of Galieno, the Cathedral, and the Arena or Roman Amphitheatre, leaving by afternoon train for Venice. (*Hotel Victoria.*)

Wednesday, August 3d.
Thursday, August 4th.
{ **IN VENICE,** during which time gondolas will be provided for visiting the most important points of interest, including the Church of St. Marc, Royal Palace, the Palace of the Doges, the Bridge of Sighs, State Prisons, the principal Churches, Museums, Art Galleries, the Islands of the Lagoons, the Lido, etc., etc.

Friday, August 5th.—Leave by noon train for Florence, via Bologna. (*Hotel d'Europe.*)

The Railway line between Bologna and Florence, which intersects the Tuscan Apennines, is one of the grandest in Europe. Bridges, tunnels (45 in all), and galleries are traversed in uninterrupted succession. Beautiful views are obtained of the valleys and gorges of the Apennines, and of the luxuriant plains of Tuscany, "the Garden of Italy."

Saturday, August 6th.
Sunday, August 7th.
{ **IN FLORENCE,** during which time visits will be made to the Tombs of the Medicis, the Cathedral and Baptistry, Church of Santa Croce (the Westminster Abbey of Italy), the Uffizi Gallery, Palaces of the Signoria and Pitti, etc., etc.

Monday, August 8th.—By morning express train, *via* Torontola and Chiusi, to Rome. (*Hotel d'Allemagne.*)

Tuesday, August 9th.
Wednesday, August 10th.
Thursday, August 11th.
Friday, August 12th.
{ **IN ROME,** three days of which will be devoted to carriage excursions, under the superintendence of Mr. Shakspere Wood, the eminent archaeologist, according to the following programme.

N. B.—Special attention is called to the fact that, under an agreement between Mr. Shakspere Wood *and ourselves, our parties are the* ONLY *ones that do the sight-seeing of Rome under his charge.*

FIRST DAY.

The Palatine.—The Seven Hills; remains of the Walls of Romulus and Port Mugonia; remains of Temples and Edifices of the early Republic; remains of Houses of the Republican period; House of Tiberius Claudius Nero, with fresco paintings.

The Palace of the Cæsars.—Site of the House of Augustus: Palace of Tiberius; substructions of the Palace of Caligula, and Porticos built by him to the Domus Tiberiana; great suite of State rooms built by Domitian; Lararium, Basilica, Triclinium, etc. ; Intermontium; great Stadium of Domitian; gigantic Porticos of Septimius Severus; site of Septizonium, etc., etc.

Basilica of Constantine.

Arch of Titus.—Bas-relief of Soldiers carrying Seven-branched Candlesticks, etc.

(AFTER LUNCH.)

The Colosseum.
Temple of Venus and Rome.
Remains of Domus Transitoria of Nero.
Arch of Constantine.
Meta Sudans.
Temple of Vesta.

The Pantheon.
Temple of Fortuna Virilis.
Ponte Rotto and View along the Tiber.
The Cloaca Maxima.
Theatre of Marcellus.
The Portico of Otavia.

SECOND DAY.

THE FORUM ROMANUM.—Via Sacra; Vicus Tuscus; Clivus Capitulinus; Temples of Castor and Pollux, the Deified Julius, Saturn, Vespasian, Concord; the Basilica Julia, Honorary Monuments, the Pedestal of Domitian's Statue, Column of Phocas; Rostrum; Arch of Septimius Severus; Portico of the Dei Cousentes; the Tabularium.

THE TARPÆIAN ROCK, THE MAMERTINE PRISON, THE FORA OF THE EMPERORS AUGUSTUS, NERO, TRAJAN.

(AFTER LUNCH.)

THE GOLDEN HOUSE OF NERO, BATHS OF TITUS,

BASILICA OF ST. CLEMENT; the Basilica of the Twelfth Century; the now subterranean Basilica of the Fourth Century; marvelously preserved Frescoes; House of Clement: Temple of Mithras; remains of a grand edifice of the Republican period, superimposed on a portion of the wall of the Kings, beneath the subterranean Basilica.

BASILICA OF ST. JOHN LATERAN, THE SCALA SANCTA, AQUEDUCT OF NERO, BASILICA OF ST. PAUL, Outside the Walls.

THIRD DAY.

VATICAN MUSEUM OF SCULPTURE.

THE SIXTINE CHAPEL. Michael Angelo's "Last Judgment."

STANZE AND LOGGIE OF RAPHAEL.

VATICAN PICTURE GALLERY.—"The Transfiguration;" "Communion of St. Jerome;" "Madonna di Foligno," etc., etc.

(AFTER LUNCH.)

BATHS OF CARACALLA, PORTA ST. SEBASTIANO, COLOMBARIA.

THE APPIAN WAY.—Tombs of Geta, Priscilla, Cecilia Metella, Seneca, the Cotta Family, etc., etc.; Tumuli of the Horatii and Curiatii; the Villa of the Quintilii, the Ustrinum; the Circus of Romulus; the Catacombs. (See "New Guide to Ancient and Modern Rome," price $2.00.)

N. B.—During the stay in Rome a pleasant Excursion can be made by Steam Tramway to TIVOLI. Excursion tickets may be had at Cook's Tourist Office, 1 B. Piazza di Spagna; price $1.

Saturday, August 13th.—Leave by morning train for Naples. (Grand Hotel Nobile.)

Sunday, August 14th. ⎫   IN NAPLES, during which time the party will visit
Monday, August 15th. ⎬   the principal places of interest in the city and sur-
Tuesday, August 16th. ⎭   roundings, including a carriage excursion to Pompeii and Herculaneum.

Wednesday, August 17th.—Leave Naples by early morning express train, via Rome, for Pisa. (Hotel de Londres.)

Thursday, August 18th.—The morning will be spent in PISA viewing the Cathedral, Baptistry, Leaning Tower, Campo Santo, etc., leaving by noon train by the Riviera Railway for Genoa. (Hotel de la Ville.)

Friday, August 19th.—IN GENOA, visiting the Cathedral, Church of the Annunziata, Palace of the Doges, Public Gardens, etc.

Saturday, August 20th.—Leave by noon train for Turin. (Hotel Trombetta.)

Places of interest are the Royal Palace, Museums, Cathedral, Squares, etc.

Sunday, August 21st.—A day of rest IN TURIN.

Monday, August 22d.—Leave by morning train for Milan. (Grand Hotel de Milan.)

Tuesday, August 23d.—IN MILAN, visiting the Cathedral dedicated to Marie Nascenti, one of the finest specimens of Gothic architecture in the world;

the Gallery Vittorio Emanuele or Public Arcade, which is one of the most spacious and attractive of its kind in existence ; the Arch of Peace, the Brera Collection of Pictures and Statues, the Church of Santa Maria delle Grazie, containing, in the Monastery, the celebrated "Last Supper" of Leonardo da Vinci, etc.

Wednesday, August 24th.—Leave by morning train for **ARONA**, situated on the shores of the beautiful Lake Maggiore. (*Hotel d'Italie et de la Poste.*) Leaving same evening by diligence for Brieg.

Thursday, August 25th.—Through the magnificent and historic **SIMPLON PASS**, arriving at Brieg at 4.10 p. m. (*Hotel des Couronnes et Poste.*)

Friday, August 26th.—Leave Brieg by Simplon Railway for **MARTIGNY**. (*Hotel Clerc.*)

Saturday, August 27th.—Go by mules or carriages over the **TETE NOIR** to Chamounix. (*Hotel d'Angleterre.*)

Sunday, August 28. Monday, August 29.	**IN THE VALLEY OF THE CHAMOUNIX.** The hotel here commands a magnificent view of MONT BLANC. Excursions may be made to the Montanvert, Mauvais Pas, Mer de Glace, Chapeau, Jardin, Flegere, or to the beautiful gorges of LA DIOZA.

Tuesday, August 30th.—Leave by diligence through Sallanches for Geneva.

Wednesday, August 31st.—**IN GENEVA.** Visits will be made to the Cathedral where Calvin preached, the Russian Church, Rath's Museum, Rousseau's Island, the Meeting of the Waters, etc.

Thursday, September 1st.—Leave Geneva by morning train for **BERNE**, stopping over a train at Fribourg (if considered advisable by the conductor). (*Hotel Bellevue.*) A magnificent panorama of the snowy peaks of the Bernese Alps may be seen from the garden of the Hotel, or from the terrace of the Cathedral, on a fine day. The Cathedral (1421-1573) contains a celebrated organ, on which evening recitals are given. The Clock Tower, Bear Pit, Kindli-fresser, Gothic Church, Rathhaus, etc., constitute the sight-seeing of the capital of Switzerland.

Friday, September 2d.—Leave Berne by morning express train for **INTER-LACKEN**, one of the most beautiful spots in Switzerland, and in full view of the Jungfrau. (*Hotel Victoria.*)

Saturday, September 3d. Sunday, September 4th.	**IN INTERLACKEN.** Carriages will be provided for an excursion to Grindelwald, to see the wonderful Glaciers. Short and pleasant walks may be made to Heimwehfluh, Unspunnen, Beatenberg, Thurnberg, etc., most of which places afford good views of the Lakes of Thun and Brienz. An excursion can be made from here to the celebrated **GIESSBACH FALLS** at a trifling expense.

Monday, September 5th.—By rail and steamer to Brienz, and by carriage over the picturesque **BRUNIG PASS** to Alpnacht, passing through Lungern and Sarnen, and by the Lake of that name (4½ miles long), taking steamer at Alpnacht, on the Lake of the Four Cantons, to Lucerne. (*Swan Hotel.*)

Tuesday, September 6th. Wednesday, September 7th.	**IN LUCERNE,** during which time an excursion on Lake Lucerne and the ascent of the Righi will be made.

At Lucerne may be visited the Lion cut in solid rock, after design, by Thorwaldsen, in memory of the Swiss Guards who fell in defending Louis XVI. against the revolutionary mob in Paris, August 10th, 1792. The Glacier Garden, in which are many relics of lacustrine habitations, etc., adjoins the "Lion." The Cathedral, containing one of the best organs in Switzerland, and the quaint Church-yard, are full of interest. Old Bridges and Fortifications. The Lake of Lucerne (*Vierwaldstaedtersee*) is full of wild and picturesque scenery, and is associated with the legend of William Tell.

Thursday, September 8th.—Proceed by morning train, *via* Bale, to **PARIS.** (*Hotel to be arranged.*) *Baggage examined at Delle or Paris.*

Friday, September 9th.
Saturday, September 10th.
Sunday, September 11th.
Monday, September 12th.

{ **IN PARIS,** three days of which will be devoted to carriage drives, visiting the principal places of interest in and around the city, including an excursion to St. Cloud, Sèvres and Versailles, according to programme of First Section, on pages 37 and 38.

Tuesday, September 13th.—Leave by night service, *via* Rouen, Dieppe and Newhaven, for London. (*Midland Grand Hotel.*) *Baggage examined at Newhaven.*

Passengers preferring the short sea mail route via Calais and Dover can be supplied with tickets for that route on payment of the difference of fare.

Wednesday, September 14th.—**IN LONDON.** Leaving by evening express train for Glasgow (*Cockburn Hotel.*)

Thursday, September 15th.—Leave **GLASGOW** or Greenock by Anchor Line steamer for New York.

Sunday, September 25th.—Expect to arrive at **NEW YORK.**

THE PRICE FOR THE THIRD SECTION IS $500,

WHICH INCLUDES

First-class Ocean passage both ways,	22 Days.
First-class Hotel accommodation in Great Britain,	11 Days.
First-class Hotel accommodation on the Continent,	55 Days.
	Total, 88 Days.

IT ALSO INCLUDES :

First-class railway and steamboat traveling for the entire journey; omnibuses and porterage between stations and hotels; free transportation of 60 lbs. of baggage; gratuities to servants; carriages to Abbotsford; gondolas for one day in Venice; three days' carriages in Rome and the services of Mr. Shakspere Wood; carriage trip to Pompeii; carriage excursion to Grindelwald; excursion on Lake Lucerne and ascent of the Righi; three days' carriage drives in Paris; fees for sight-seeing, as per Conductor's programme; services of special local guides when necessary, and also the services of the Conductor, who acts as Interpreter and Manager.

NOTE.—*The Conductor will only pay for carriages ordered by himself, and the services of the guides will be for the whole party.*

Hotel provision for each country to be according to the custom of the country, viz.: in Great Britain, meat breakfast, table d'hote dinner, tea, bedroom, lights, service and attendance. On the Continent: Meat breakfast, dinner at table d'hote (with or without wine, as the Hotel provides), bedroom, lights and service.

SPECIAL NOTICE.—Each person joining this party will also receive an admission ticket to the AMERICAN EXCHANGE IN EUROPE, free of charge, entitling the holder to all the privileges of the Exchange while the party is in London. For particulars see page 64.

STEAMSHIP ACCOMMODATION.

We have a good selection of staterooms provided for this party, mostly outside rooms, and, with the exception of a few forward rooms (where three passengers will be placed), all the rooms in the after-part of the ship will be occupied by *two persons only.*

A DEPOSIT OF FIFTY DOLLARS

is required from each person who decides to go with this party; when the deposit is made, the name is registered, and the berths are allotted in the exact order of these deposits, the earliest depositors, of course, receiving the best berths.

Forty dollars of this deposit may be withdrawn up to June 15th, after which time the whole amount is due.

HOW TO JOIN THE PARTY.

Persons desirous of joining this party should write as early as possible, enclosing draft on any bank or postal order made payable to the order of Thos. Cook & Son, *and stating which Section they wish to join.* We will, upon receipt of the same, return a "Deposit Receipt" and a plan of the steamer, showing the location of the berths we can offer. Should the choice of berths be left to us, we will use our best judgment in the interest of each, and advise them at once. The balance of the money can be paid any time after June 15th.

SIZE OF SECTIONS.

In order to insure comfort, and secure good accommodation at Hotels, the number of passengers in each section, after leaving London, will not exceed THIRTY.

EXTENSION OF TIME.

Breaks in the Journey can be made at almost any point, and as the return steamship tickets are good for one year, any of the members of this party can remain in Europe at their discretion. The whole amount of fare must be paid before starting, but they can receive back the value of their unused tickets and Hotel coupons, less 10 per cent. (*Swiss Traveling Tickets excepted*), at the Chief London Office, or they can be exchanged for tickets to other points, at their full value.

On the return from the Continent, if any wish to extend their tour to the English Lakes, Scotland and Ireland, taking the steamer at Liverpool or Queenstown, quotations will be given by Messrs. Thos. Cook & Son; and if a party of 10 or more is made up for such supplementary tour, a Conductor will be sent with them, without extra charge.

HOMEWARD ATLANTIC VOYAGE.

We have proved from experience that a large percentage of the passengers booked for Personally Conducted Parties do not return by the Atlantic steamers on the exact dates given in these itineraries, therefore we must impress upon the members of this party the importance of giving us the earliest possible notice and the date they intend leaving for New York, so that good berths may be secured for them.

Passengers failing to do this will have to take their own risk as to the location of berths that may be allotted them, when they finally give instructions for their return passage to be secured.

OTHER LINES OF STEAMERS.

Any who desire to avail themselves of this Tour, but prefer some other line of steamers, we can accommodate them, and will give them a special quotation either higher or lower, according to the line preferred. We will also, for those who have engaged steamship passage, give quotations, and book them from Liverpool, Glasgow, London or Paris.

DETOURS.

Any member will be allowed to leave the party to visit other localities, provided early notice be given to the Conductor, so that engagements for hotel accommodation may not be violated. Hotel coupons will be supplied to those who so leave the party for the number of days they expect to be absent. Any unused coupons to be redeemed at the advertised rate. No allowance can, however, be made for incidental expenses when not traveling with the Conductor.

BAGGAGE.

Whilst anxious to render all possible assistance to travelers in the transport, care and registration of baggage, Thos. Cook & Son cannot admit responsibility in cases of detention, stray conveyance, damage to or loss of baggage. In all cases of transference it is necessary that baggage should be identified by its owners, especially on entering and leaving hotels and railway stations ; and whenever baggage is subject to customs examination, its owners should be present to answer for it.

Great care will be taken in the registration and conveyance of the trunks or portmanteaus of the parties whilst traveling with the Conductor ; but it must be distinctly understood that all small packages, such as hand-bags, umbrella's, traveling rugs, &c., must remain entirely under the control of the passenger.

LABELS for large baggage and hand baggage for the use of the members of this party will be furnished by us upon application.

LETTERS may be addressed to any member of the party, care of THOMAS COOK & SON, LUDGATE CIRCUS, LONDON, and such letters will be carefully forwarded to the Conductor of the party for delivery.

LETTERS OF CREDIT AND CIRCULAR CHECKS are issued by us at current rates, in the denomination of five or ten pounds sterling each, and are payable at nearly every point on the route, or will be cashed by the Conductor as required, in the currency of the country where the party happens to be at the time. They are also cashed at the AMERICAN EXCHANGE IN EUROPE, No. 449 Strand, London, W. C.

CAUTIONARY PROVISO.

The liability of Alpine roads and railroads in the neighborhood of mountains to damage from storms and other influences beyond human control, renders it necessary that we should announce that we cannot be responsible for detention or expenses incurred by deviation of routes occasioned by circumstances of this nature, nor for delays or deviations that may be caused through the railways being required for military purposes.

The most that Companies will do under such circumstances is to repay the value of any tickets or proportion of tickets not used for lines thus rendered impassable; and all claims in such cases must be sent in writing, accompanied by the unused tickets, within one month from the date for which such tickets were available.

THOS. COOK & SON,

P. O. Box 4197.   261 Broadway, New York.

Autumnal Tours
to
Egypt and Palestine.

In reply to the many inquiries we are receiving, asking for information in regard to the best season for traveling through the Holy Land, we may state that the best months to visit Palestine are the months of March, April and May, when every thing is fresh and green; and that we do not recommend traveling through that country at other periods. In June, July, August and September it is too hot, and serious risk is run by Americans attempting to make the journey. In October the cool winds make traveling more endurable, but still the country is dusty, dry and parched, and not seen at its best; there is, however, less risk of malaria and disease.

In December the rains come, which usually last through the Winter months, making traveling an impossibility.

We may also add that since the commencement of our Palestine Tours, we have never known a party to travel through that country in the Autumn, without some of the passengers being ill of fever, and very often one or more of them succumb and have to be left behind.

Our complete programmes for Palestine are issued in November or December, and provide for extended travel during the months of March, April and May, and at this season more people visit Palestine than at any other.

From the experience of past years we are aware that a certain number of Americans are compelled either to travel through Egypt and Palestine in the Autumn, or deprive themselves of the pleasure of the tour, and we are prepared to give every information and assistance to any person contemplating such a tour.

Our ordinary custom is to organize special parties to go through the country from Jaffa to Jerusalem, the Jordan, Dead Sea, over the Lebanon to Damascus, Baalbeck, coming out of the country at Beyrout, taking steamer for Smyrna, Constantinople, Athens, etc. This is our Spring arrangement, and under it we visit Egypt first.

In the Autumn, all these arrangements are necessarily reversed, and our plan is to go into Palestine at Beyrout, and go south with the weather, visiting Egypt last.

In this connection we may state, that since our first Palestine announcements were published, we have conveyed more than 2,500 travelers for short and long tours through the country, and that more than *three-fourths* of the English and American visitors to the country last Winter (1879-'80), were traveling under our arrangements; and at the present time we are conveying, *en route* to or from Egypt and Palestine, the largest number of passengers we have ever had to convey at any one season.

Our chief representatives and staffs at Jaffa and Jerusalem have the respect of officials and of the native population, and amongst the Bedouins there are few who would venture to molest them, and to our Manager there we have committed the entire local arrangements, whilst we acknowledge, most directly, our home and foreign responsibilities to all who accept our proposals.

Our tent equipments are of the best possible description, and the largest collection in the country, and we employ two members of our staff during the summer months in repairing and keeping in good order everything for the Winter season.

The horses we employ are the best to be found in the country, and our contracts for horses and mules are made direct with the sheikhs of the muleteers of the different districts.

The provisions supplied are of the best possible description, and we have received many commendatory testimonials as to the skill displayed by our cooks whilst in camp, but we have never yet received a single complaint against them.

The coming Autumn it is our intention to respond to the applications for Palestine travel, and will offer the opportunity to visit the country by **Either a Long or Short Tour**, as may be desired.

These parties will leave London in the latter part of September, traveling *via* Paris, Turin and Rome, and arrangements can be made for intending travelers to join these parties at almost any point *en route*. Fares and full particulars will be given upon application to

THOS. COOK & SON,
261 Broadway, New York.

ANNUAL MAY PARTY.

April.	Wednesday	27	.... Leave New York
May.	Sunday	8	.... Due in Liverpool
	Monday	9	.... To London
	Tuesday	10	.... In London
	Wednesday	11	.... do
	Thursday	12	.... do
	Friday	13	.... do
	Saturday	14	.... do
	Sunday	15	.... do
	Monday	16	.... To Paris
	Tuesday	17	.... Arr. Paris
	Wednesday	18	.... In Paris
	Thursday	19	.... do
	Friday	20	.... do
	Saturday	21	.... do
	Sunday	22	.... do
	Monday	23	.... To Turin
	Tuesday	24	.... Arr. Turin
	Wednesday	25	.... To Genoa
	Thursday	26	.... In Genoa
	Friday	27	.... To Pisa
	Saturday	28	.... To Rome
	Sunday	29	.... In Rome
	Monday	30	.... do
	Tuesday	31	.... do
June.	Wednesday	1	.... do
	Thursday	2	.... To Naples
	Friday	3	.... In Naples
	Saturday	4	.... do
	Sunday	5	.... do
	Monday	6	.... do
	Tuesday	7	.... To Rome
	Wednesday	8	.... To Florence
	Thursday	9	.... In Florence
	Friday	10	.... do
	Saturday	11	.... To Venice
	Sunday	12	.... In Venice
	Monday	13	.... do
	Tuesday	14	.... do
	Wednesday	15	.... To Milan
	Thursday	16	.... In Milan
	Friday	17	.... do
	Saturday	18	.... To Stresa
	Sunday	19	.... At Stresa
	Monday	20	.... To Brigue
	Tuesday	21	.... To Martigny
	Wednesday	22	.... To Chamounix
	Thursday	23	.... In Chamounix
	Friday	24	.... do
	Saturday	25	.... To Geneva
	Sunday	26	.... In Geneva
	Monday	27	.... To Berne
	Tuesday	28	.... To Interlacken
	Wednesday	29	.... To Grindelwald
	Thursday	30	.... To Glessbach
July.	Friday	1	.... To Lucerne
	Saturday	2	.... In Lucerne
	Sunday	3	.... do
	Monday	4	.... To Zurich
	Tuesday	5	.... To Neuhausen
	Wednesday	6	.... To Strasbourg
	Thursday	7	.... To Baden Baden
	Friday	8	.... To Heidelberg
	Saturday	9	.... To Wiesbaden
	Sunday	10	.... In Wiesbaden .
	Monday	11	.... To Cologne
	Tuesday	12	.... To Brussels
	Wednesday	13	.... In Brussels
	Thursday	14	.... do
	Friday	15	.... To Antwerp
	Saturday	16	.... To the Hague
	Sunday	17	.... At the Hague
	Monday	18	.... To Amsterdam
	Tuesday	19	.... In Amsterdam
	Wednesday	20	.... To London
	Thursday	21	.... In London
	Friday	22	.... To Liverpool
	Saturday	23	.... Leave for New York
Aug.	Wednesday	3	.... Due in New York

THE JUNE PARTY.

June.	Saturday	11	.... Leave New York
	Monday	20	.... Due at Queenstown
	Tuesday	21	.... To Glengariff
	Wednesday	22	.... To Killarney
	Thursday	23	.... At Killarney
	Friday	24	.... do
	Saturday	25	.... To Dublin
	Sunday	26	.... In Dublin
	Monday	27	.... To Loudonderry
	Tuesday	28	.... To Portrush
	Wednesday	29	.... To Glasgow
	Thursday	30	.... To Inversnaid
July.	Friday	1	.... To Edinburgh
	Saturday	2	.... In Edinburgh
	Sunday	3	.... do
	Monday	4	.... To London
	Tuesday	5	.... In London
	Wednesday	6	.... do
	Thursday	7	.... do
	Friday	8	.... To Rotterdam
	Saturday	9	.... To Amsterdam
	Sunday	10	.... In Amsterdam
	Monday	11	.... To Antwerp
	Tuesday	12	.... To Brussels
	Wednesday	13	.... In Brussels
	Thursday	14	.... do
	Friday	15	.... To Cologne
	Saturday	16	.... To Wiesbaden
	Sunday	17	.... In Wiesbaden
	Monday	18	.... To Heidelberg
	Tuesday	19	.... In Heidelberg
	Wednesday	20	.... To Neuhausen
	Thursday	21	.... To Zurich
	Friday	22	.... To Lucerne
	Saturday	23	.... In Lucerne
	Sunday	24	.... do
	Monday	25	.... To Glessbach
	Tuesday	26	.... To Interlacken
	Wednesday	27	.... In Interlacken
	Thursday	28	.... do
	Friday	29	.... To Berne
	Saturday	30	.... To Ouchy
	Sunday	31	.... At Ouchy
Aug.	Monday	1	.... To Martigny
	Tuesday	2	.... To Chamounix
	Wednesday	3	.... In Chamounix
	Thursday	4	.... To Geneva
	Friday	5	.... To Paris
	Saturday	6	.... Arr. Paris
	Sunday	7	.... In Paris
	Monday	8	.... do
	Tuesday	9	.... do
	Wednesday	10	.... do
	Thursday	11	.... do
	Friday	12	.... To London
	Saturday	13	.... In London
	Sunday	14	.... do
	Monday	15	.... To Liverpool
	Tuesday	16	.... Leave for New York
	Saturday	27	.... Due in New York

ITALIAN EXTENSION.

Same Itinerary as above to Geneva.

Aug.	Friday	5	.... To Turin
	Saturday	6	.... To Milan
	Sunday	7	.... In Milan
	Monday	8	.... To Venice
	Tuesday	9	.... In Venice
	Wednesday	10	.... do
	Thursday	11	.... To Florence
	Friday	12	.... In Florence
	Saturday	13	.... To Naples
	Sunday	14	.... In Naples
	Monday	15	.... do
	Tuesday	16	.... To Rome
	Wednesday	17	.... In Rome
	Thursday	18	.... do
	Friday	19	.... To Pisa
	Saturday	20	.... To Genoa
	Sunday	21	.... In Genoa
	Monday	22	.... To Paris
	Tuesday	23	.... In Paris
	Wednesday	24	.... do
	Thursday	25	.... do
	Friday	26	.... do
	Saturday	27	.... To London
	Sunday	28	.... In London
	Monday	29	.... To Liverpool
	Tuesday	30	.... Leave for New York
Sept.	Saturday	10	.... Due in New York

ANNUAL VACATION PARTY.

FIRST SECTION.

July.	Sat.	2	Leave N. Y.
	Wed.	13	Due in Glasgow
	Thurs.	14	To Edinburgh
	Fri.	15	In Edinburgh
	Sat.	16	To London
	Sun.	17	In London
	Mon.	18	do
	Tues.	19	do
	Wed.	20	To Antwerp
	Thurs.	21	To Brussels
	Fri.	22	In Brussels
	Sat.	23	To Cologne
	Sun.	24	In Cologne
	Mon.	25	To Mayence
	Tues.	26	To Heidelberg
	Wed.	27	In Heidelberg
	Thurs.	28	To Bale
	Fri.	29	To Lucerne
	Sat.	30	In Lucerne
	Sun.	31	do
Aug.	Mon.	1	To Giessbach
	Tues.	2	To Interlacken
	Wed.	3	To Berne
	Thurs.	4	To Lausanne
	Fri.	5	To Martigny
	Sat.	6	To Chamounix
	Sun.	7	In Chamounix
	Mon.	8	do
	Tues.	9	To Geneva
	Wed.	10	To Paris
	Thurs.	11	In Paris
	Fri.	12	do
	Sat.	13	do
	Sun.	14	do
	Mon.	15	do
	Tues.	16	To London
	Wed.	17	To Glasgow
	Thurs.	18	Leave for N. Y.
	Sun.	28	Due in N. Y.

SECOND SECTION.

July.	Sat.	2	Leave N. Y.
	Wed.	13	Due in Glasgow
	Thurs.	14	To Edinburgh
	Fri.	15	In Edinburgh
	Sat.	16	To London
	Sun.	17	In London
	Mon.	18	do
	Tues.	19	do
	Wed.	20	To Antwerp
	Thurs.	21	To Brussels
	Fri.	22	In Brussels
	Sat.	23	To Cologne
	Sun.	24	In Cologne
	Mon.	25	To Mayence
	Tues.	26	To Heidelberg
	Wed.	27	In Heidelberg
	Thurs.	28	To Bale
	Fri.	29	To Lucerne
	Sat.	30	In Lucerne
	Sun.	31	do
Aug.	Mon.	1	To Giessbach
	Tues.	2	To Interlacken
	Wed.	3	To Berne
	Thurs.	4	To Lausanne
	Fri.	5	To Martigny
	Sat.	6	To Chamounix
	Sun.	7	In Chamounix
	Mon.	8	do
	Tues.	9	To Geneva
	Wed.	10	In Geneva
	Thurs.	11	To Turin
	Fri.	12	To Milan
	Sat.	13	To Venice
	Sun.	14	In Venice
	Mon.	15	do
	Tues.	16	To Florence
	Wed.	17	In Florence
	Thurs.	18	To Rome
	Fri.	19	In Rome
	Sat.	20	do
	Sun.	21	do
	Mon.	22	To Pisa
	Tues.	23	To Genoa
	Wed.	24	In Genoa
	Thurs.	25	To Paris
	Fri.	26	In Paris
	Sat.	27	do
	Sun.	28	do
	Mon.	29	do
	Tues.	30	To London
	Wed.	31	To Glasgow
Sept.	Thurs.	1	Leave for N. Y.
	Sun.	11	Due in N. Y.

THIRD SECTION.

July.	Sat.	2	Leave N. Y.
	Wed.	13	Due in Glasgow
	Thurs.	14	To Edinburgh
	Fri.	15	In Edinburgh
	Sat.	16	To London
	Sun.	17	In London
	Mon.	18	do
	Tues.	19	do
	Wed.	20	do
	Thurs.	21	To Antwerp
	Fri.	22	To Brussels
	Sat.	23	In Brussels
	Sun.	24	do
	Mon.	25	To Cologne
	Tues.	26	To Mayence
	Wed.	27	To Heidelberg
	Thurs.	28	In Heidelberg
	Fri.	29	To Munich
	Sat.	30	In Munich
	Sun.	31	do
Aug.	Mon.	1	To Verona
	Tues.	2	To Venice
	Wed.	3	In Venice
	Thurs.	4	do
	Fri.	5	To Florence
	Sat.	6	In Florence
	Sun.	7	do
	Mon.	8	To Rome
	Tues.	9	In Rome
	Wed.	10	do
	Thurs.	11	do
	Fri.	12	do
	Sat.	13	To Naples
	Sun.	14	In Naples
	Mon.	15	do
	Tues.	16	do
	Wed.	17	To Pisa
	Thurs.	18	To Genoa
	Fri.	19	In Genoa
	Sat.	20	To Turin
	Sun.	21	In Turin
	Mon.	22	To Milan
	Tues.	23	In Milan
	Wed.	24	To Arona
	Thurs.	25	To Brigue
	Fri.	26	To Martigny
	Sat.	27	To Chamounix
	Sun.	28	In Chamounix
	Mon.	29	do
	Tues.	30	To Geneva
	Wed.	31	In Geneva
Sept.	Thurs.	1	To Berne
	Fri.	2	To Interlacken
	Sat.	3	In Interlacken
	Sun.	4	do
	Mon.	5	To Lucerne
	Tues.	6	In Lucerne
	Wed.	7	do
	Thurs.	8	To Paris
	Fri.	9	In Paris
	Sat.	10	do
	Sun.	11	do
	Mon.	12	do
	Tues.	13	To London
	Wed.	14	To Glasgow
	Thurs.	15	Leave for N. Y.
	Sun.	25	Due in N. Y.

A FEW USEFUL PHRASES FOR THE USE OF TOURISTS.

ENGLISH.	FRENCH.	GERMAN.	ITALIAN.
Yes. If you please.	Oui. S'il vous plaît.	Ja. Ich bitte.	Sì. Se vi piace.
No. Thank you.	Non. Merci.	Nein. Ich danke.	No. Vi ringrazio.
I am— Are you—?	Je suis— Etes vous—?	Ich bin— Sind Sie—?	Io sono— Siete—?
I have— Have you—?	J'ai— Avez-vous—?	Ich habe. Haben Sie—?	Io ho— Avete—?
I will not— Will you—?	Je ne veux pas— Vendez-vous—?	Ich will nicht— Verkaufen Sie—?	Non voglio— Volete—?
I want— Do you sell—?	J'ai besoin de— Vendez-vous—?	Ich brauche— Verkaufen Sie—?	Ho bisogno— Vendete—?
Say only, 'Yes' or 'No.'	Dites seulement 'oui' ou 'non.'	Sagen Sie nur 'ja' oder 'nein.'	Dica solamente 'sì' o 'no.'
Write it. Give me—	Ecrivez-le. Donnez-moi—.	Schreiben Sie— Geben Sie mir—.	Scrivete. Datemi.
Monday. Tuesday. Wednesday.	Lundi. Mardi. Mercredi.	Montag. Dienstag. Mittwoch.	Lunedì. Martedì. Mercoledì.
Thursday. Friday. Saturday.	Jeudi. Vendredi. Samedi.	Donnerstag. Freitag. Samstag.	Giovedì. Venerdì. Sabato.
Sunday. To-day. To-morrow.	Dimanche. Aujourd'hui. Demain.	Sonntag. Heute. Morgen.	Domenica. Oggi. Dimani.
One, two, three, four, five, six, seven, eight	Un, deux, trois, quatre, cinq, six, sept, huit	Ein, zwei, drei, vier, fünf, sechs, sieben	Uno, due, tre, quattro, cinque, sei
Nine, ten, eleven, twelve.	Neuf, dix, onze, douze.	Acht, neun, zehn, elf, zwölf.	Sette, otto, nove, dieci, undici, dodici.
On the Road.			
Where is—? Is there a house?	Où est—? Y a-t-il une maison?	Wo ist—? Ist ein Haus dort?	Dov'è—? C'è una casa?
How far to—?	Combien de distance à—?	Wie weit nach—?	Quanto è distante a—?
Are you going to—?	Allez-vous à—?	Gehen Sie nach—?	Va ella a—?
Show me the way to—.	Indiquez-moi à—.	Zeigen Sie mir den Weg nach—.	Indicatemi—.
Is it easy to find?	Trouve-t-on facilement?	Ist es leicht zu finden?	È facile a trovarsi?
Must I go to the right, left, straight on?	Faut-il aller à droite, à gauche, tout droit?	Muss ich rechts geben, links, gerade aus?	Debbo voltarmi poi a destra, a sinistra, diritto?
Road. Foot-path.	Chemin. Sentier.	Weg. Fussweg.	Via. Sentiero.
What is the name of this place?	Quel est le nom de ce lieu?	Wie heisst dieser Ort?	Come si chiama quel paese?
How many hours' walk? (1 hr.—3 mls.).	Combien de lieues?	Wie viel Stunden?	Quante ore?
Will you carry? I will give—.	Voulez vous porter? Je donnerai—.	Wollen Sie tragen? Ich will geben—.	Vuole portare? Darò—.
Stop! Go on! Slowly. Quickly.	Arrêtez! Allez! Lentement. Vite.	Halt! Vorwärts! Langsam. Schnell	Fermatevi. Su via! Adagio. Presto.
On the Rail.			
Railway. Station. First-class.	Chemin de fer. Gare. Premier.	Eisenbahn. Bahnhof. Erster Klasse.	Strada ferrata. Stazione. Prima classe.
Porter. My luggage. Goods train.	Facteur. Mon bagage. Train de marchandises	Träger. Mein Gepäck. Güterzug.	Facchino. Mio bagaglio. Treno merci.
At what o'clock does it depart?	A quelle heure part-il?	Um wie viel Uhr fährt er ab?	A che ora parte?
Do we change carriages here?	Change-t-on des voitures ici?	Wechselt man die Wagen hier?	Si cambia qui le carrozze?
How long do we stop here?	Combien de temps nous arrêtons-nous ici?	Wie lange halten wir hier?	Quanto tempo ci fermiamo qui?
In a Town.			
Passport. Post. Prepaid.	Passeport. Poste. Affranchie.	Pass. Post. Frei.	Passaporto. Posta. Franco.
Custom-house. Office. Bank.	Douane. Bureau. Banque.	Zollamt. Bureau. Bank.	Dogana. Uffizio. Banca.
Street. Bridge. Cathedral. Church	Rue. Pont. Cathédrale. Eglise.	Strasse. Brücke. Dom. Kirche.	Strada. Ponte. Cattedrale. Chiesa.
Hotel. Coffee-house. Confectioner.	Hôtel. Café. Confiseur.	Gasthof. Kaffeehaus. Conditor.	Albergo. Caffè. Confetturiere.
Shop. Theatre. Baths.	Boutique. Théâtre. Bains.	Laden. Theater. Badehaus.	Bottega. Teatro. Bagni.
Where does he live?	...où demeure-t-il?	Wo wohnt—?	Dove abita—?
Have you a letter for me?	Avez vous une lettre pour moi?	Haben Sie einen Brief für mich?	Avete una lettera per me?
How much does it cost?	Combien coûte-elle?	Wie viel kostet?	Quanto costa?
It is too much. Here it is!	C'est trop. La voilà!	Ist zu viel. Ist hier!	È troppo. Ecco.
At a Hotel.			
Landlord. Waiter. Chambermaid.	Maître d'hôtel. Garçon. Femme de chambre	Gastwirth. Kellner. Zimmermagd.	Albergatore. Cameriere. Cameriera.
Show me a room.	Montrez-moi une chambre.	Zeigen Sie mir ein Zimmer.	Mostratemi una camera.
On the (first, second, third) floor.	Au (premier, second, troisième) étage	Im (ersten, zweiten, dritten) Stocke.	Al (primo, secondo, terzo) piano.
Are the sheets well aired?	Les draps, sont-ils bien secs?	Sind die Bettücher trocken?	Le lenzuola sono asciutte?
Waken me at (six) o'clock.	Réveillez-moi à (six) heures.	Wecken Sie mich um (sechs) Uhr	Mi sveglierete a (sei) ore.
Breakfast.—Tea. Coffee.	Déjeuner.—Thé. Café.	Frühstück.—Thee. Kaffee.	Colazione.—Tè. Caffè.
Sugar. Milk. Bread. Butter.	Sucre. Lait. Pain. Beurre.	Zucker. Milch. Brod. Butter.	Zucchero. Latte. Pane. Butirro.
Cutlet. Egg. Cup. Saucer.	Côtelette. Œuf. Tasse. Soucoupe.	Cotelette. Ei. Tasse. Untertasse.	Braciuola. Uova. Tazza. Sottocoppa.
Plate. Knife. Fork. Spoon.	Assiette. Couteau. Fourchette. Cuiller.	Teller. Messer. Gabel. Löffel.	Tondo. Coltello. Forchetta. Cucchiajo.
Dinner.—Soup. Fish. Salt.	Diner.—Soupe. Poisson. Sel.	Mittagessen.—Suppe. Fisch. Salz.	Pranzo.—Zuppa. Pesce. Sale.
Mutton. Beef. Fowl.	Mouton. Bœuf. Volaille.	Hammelfleisch. Rindfleisch. Geflügel.	Castrato. Manzo. Pollame.
Ham. Vegetables. Pastry. Dessert.	Jambon. Légumes. Pâtisserie. Dessert	Schinken Gemüse. Backwerk. Dessert	Prosciutto. Legumi. Pasticceria. Frutta.
A half-bottle. A glass.	Demi-bouteille. Un verre.	Halbe Flasche. Ein Glas.	Mezza-bottiglia. Uno bicchiere.
The bill.	Le compte.	Die Rechnung.	Il conto.

BRIEF DESCRIPTION

OF THE

Principal Cities and Places in Europe

VISITED BY

COOK'S

EXCURSION PARTIES FROM AMERICA.

AMSTERDAM (Holland).—Pop. 280,000. Built on a number of islands, intersected by canals. Places of interest :—Trippenhuis Museum of Paintings, 10 to 3 ; New Church, Palace, Museum van der Hoop, Old Church, Zoological Gardens, etc.

ANTWERP (Belgium).—Pop. 130,000. Situated on the River Scheldt, which is navigable for large vessels. Places of interest : Cathedral, with Rubens' "Descent from the Cross," "Elevation of the Cross," etc.; Church of St. Paul ; Hotel de Ville ; Museum ; Church of St. Jacques ; Church of the Augustines; Church of St. Andrew; Iron Pump Head, by Quintin Matsys.

BADEN BADEN (Grand Duchy of Baden).—Pop. 10,000. Prettily situated on the borders of the Black Forest, into which many interesting carriage excursions may be made. Places of interest:—Kursaal; Neue Schloss; Alte Schloss, etc.

BALE (Switzerland).—Pop. 45,000. On the Rhine, at the north-west corner of Switzerland. Places of interest:—Cathedral, with Council Hall; Museum; Hotel de Ville; Battle-field of St. Jacob, ½ mile; Battle-field of Dornach, 2 miles.

BRUSSELS (Belgium).—Pop. 262,000. This city, the capital of the Kingdom and the seat of Government. is 88 miles from Ostend, 27¼ from Antwerp, 48 from Ghent, 71½ from Liege, 92½ from Lille, 149½ from Cologne, and 215 from Paris. Places of interest:— Cathedral of St. Gudule; Galeries St. Hubert: Hotel de Ville; Museum; Royal Palace; Palace of the Duke of Arenberg; Musée Wiertz; Park; Zoological Gardens, etc. The Field of Waterloo is 12 miles from Brussels. (Cook's Tourist Office, 22, Galerie du Roi.)

BERNE (Switzerland).—Pop. 37,000. The capital of the Canton Berne, and seat of Swiss Government. Situated on the River Aar, which nearly encircles the city. Places of interest:—Cathedral, with Domplatz; Federal Palace; Museum; Clock Tower; Rathhaus; Roman Catholic Church, etc., etc.

CHAMOUNY (Savoy).—3,150 feet above the level of the sea. A village in the valley of the same name, at the foot of Mont Blanc, distant about 50 miles from Geneva. Diligences in the season. Distance from Martigny to Chamounix, 22 miles. Several days may be well devoted to explore this celebrated region. The Montanvert, which can be ascended on mules, and commands a view of the Mer de Glace, ought to be the first excursion. It is an elevated pasture on the summit of a mountain under the Aiguilles de Charmoz. From this are seen to advantage the heights of the Brevent and of the Aiguilles Rouges. At the summit of the Montanvert is a small building, where beds and refreshments may be had. The height of Montanvert above the valley of Chamounix is 2,565 feet. The Glacier de Bossons, which may be seen the same day, at the other end of the valley, is remarkable for the purity of the ice, and for the picturesque formation of its ice needles and obelisks. The Brevent, on the opposite side of the valley, 8,000 feet above the sea, affords a magnificent view of the whole range of Mont Blanc, with its numerous peaks covered with snow, and the glaciers pouring down into the valley. The Flegere, on the same side, commands the same view at a less elevation, and may be accomplished in half a day. The active mountaineer would be well repaid by a day's excursion to the Jardin, across the Mer de Glace, 9,100 feet above the sea—a small portion of green earth, covered with flowers in full bloom, in a region of snow and ice, commanding a view of the recesses of this wonderful range of snowy peaks. From Chamounix to Martigny, by the passes of the Tete Noire or the Col de Balme, about nine hours would be required. To the Jardin is a fatiguing and severe excursion for ladies. They are sometimes deceived by guides, who take them to another spot. The Tete Noire is one of the most picturesque passes in Switzerland, the rocks frequently overhanging.

COLOGNE (Germany).—This, the chief city of Rhenish Prussia, contains a population of 130,000. It is strongly fortified, and is connected with its suburb Deutz by two bridges; one a handsome iron structure, and the other, 1,250 feet in length, composed of 39 boats. The chief objects of attraction are:—the Cathedral, one of the finest Gothic churches in the world, begun in 1248; was left unfinished from the beginning of the 16th century until 1816, and finally completed in August, 1880. Nave and transept free; fee to see the choir (free only from $8\frac{1}{2}$—9 a. m.), the relics of the three Kings, and the treasury, 15 sgr.: to ascend the tower and galleries, 10 sgr.; Churches of St. Martin, St. Maria in Capitolio, St. Peter's (containing the "Crucifixion of Peter," by Rubens), St. Ursula (where the bones of the Eleven Thousand Virgins are to be seen in the walls; fee, 15 sgr). English Chapel, Bischofsgarten Strasse; Services: Sunday morning, 11; evening (summer months), 4.30 p. m. Cook's Tourist Office, 40 Domhof.

DIEPPE (France).—Pop. 26,000. A prettily-situated watering-place in Normandy. Places of interest:- Church of St. Jacques; Church of St. Reini; the Plage or Promenade overlooking the sea; the Chateau d'Arques, 3 miles, etc.

FLORENCE (Italy).—Pop. 168,000. Beautifully situated on both sides of the Arno. Places of interest :—Cathedral, with Giotto's Campanile, Brunelleschi's Cupola and the Baptistry with Ghiberti's bronze doors ; Churches of Santa Annunziata; Il Carmine; Santa Croce; San Lorenzo; Laurent de Medicis; San Marco; Santa Maria Novella; San Michele, etc. The Uffizi and Pitti palaces connected by a covered way, containing the richest collection of painting and sculptures in the world; the Palazzo Vecchio; the Palazzo Riccardi, etc.; also the Galleria Reale ; the Academy of Fine Arts; the Houses of Michael Angelo, Dante, Galileo, etc. Modern Paintings:—Societa Artistica, Viale Principe Eugenio. R. W. Spranger, Managing Director.

FRANKFORT (Germany).— Pop. 106,000. Formerly a free city, and the seat of the German Bund. Situated on the River Main, which is spanned by five bridges. Places of interest:—Town Hall ; Guttenberg Monument ; statues of Schiller and Goethe ; Cathedral; Town Library; Gallery of Paintings ; Stadel Art Institution ; Leuckenberg Museum and Library ; Bethmann Museum ; Natural History Museum; Palmengarten; Exchange, etc.

FREIBURG (Baden.)—Pop. 22,000. Situated on the River Dreisam, at the entrance to the Hollenthal (Black Forest). Places of interest:—The Cathedral or Minster; the Archbishop's Palace; and the Palace of the Grand Duke; Kaufhaus, etc. Freiburg is a convenient centre for excursions into the Black Forest.

FRIBOURG (Switzerland). Pop. 11,000. Beautifully situated on the side of a deep gorge. Places of interest:—Cathedral with famous organ, 70 stops, 7,800 pipes, generally played at noon, also a bas-relief over the entrance; great suspension bridge, 964 feet long, 186 feet high; small suspension bridge, 746 feet long, 303 feet high; Lime-tree of Fribourg opposite the ancient Rathhaus.

GENEVA (Switzerland). Pop. 56,000. Situated at the point where the River Rhone issues from the lake; 370 miles from Paris. Places of interest:— Bridge and Quai of Mont Blanc; Jardin Anglais; Isle Jean Jacques Rousseau: Tour de César; Musce Rath; Conservatoire de Musique; Hotel de Ville; Cathedral where Calvin preached; Russian Chapel; Library, etc. Cook's Tourist Office, 90 Rue du Rhône.

GENOA (Italy).—Pop. 140,000. One of the chief ports of Italy. Streets lined with marble palaces. Cathedral of San Lorenzo, very fine. Church of Annunziata. Best view of the town obtained from the Tower of Santa Maria di Carignano. Before ascending it is best to tell the Sacristan how many minutes you intend to remain, so that on descending he may open the door. The Campo Santo contains many fine monuments.

HAGUE (Holland).—Pop. 80,000. This has the reputation of being the "largest village in the world." It is the residence of the Court. Places of interest:—Palace in the Wood; Museum of medals; Museum of paintings; Bittenhof; Buitenhof; Scheveningen, a fashionable bathing place, is four miles distant.

HEIDELBERG (Baden).—Pop. 20,000. Situated on the River Neckar. The magnificent ruins of the Castle, one of the most interesting objects in Europe, occupy the hill behind the town. In a cellar under the castle is the celebrated "Tun of Heidelberg." The University is attended by about 500 students. Many charming excursions may be made in the neighborhood.

INNSBRUCK (Austrian Tyrol).--Pop. 23,000. The capital of the Tyrol, situated on the river Inn. The Franciscan Church contains the celebrated Tomb of Maximilian; the Palace; the University and the Ferdinandeum Museum are among the places of interest. The neighborhood is very beautiful.

INTERLACKEN (Switzerland).—Situated in the Canton Berne, this little town forms the chief centre for excursions in the Bernese Oberland. The hotels are for the most part very fine. Berne is reached by railway as far as Darlingen, thence by steamer to Scherzligen-Thun, and forward by railway; Lucerne is reached by railway to Bonigen, steamer to Brienz, past the celebrated Giessbach Falls, diligence over the Brunig Pass to Alpnach, and thence by steamer. Grindelwald, 12 miles from Interlacken and Lauterbrunnen, where is the Staubbach waterfall, may be easily reached by carriage. The Kursaal of Interlacken is one of the best in the country.

LONDON (England).—It is impossible to give a description of such a large city as London in this connection, but it may be here briefly stated that the population of the great Metropolis is between four and five millions, and that it is the largest and most important commercial city in the world. The principal places of interest are:—St. Paul's Cathedral; Westminster Abbey; the Tower of London, the Houses of Parliament; British Museum; Royal Exchange; Mansion House; Bank of England, etc., etc. For a description of these and other places of interest, and also for information as to how to get round the city and economize time, the traveler would do well to consult "Cook's Handbook to London;" but a more elaborate description will be found in Baedeker's Guide to London.

LAUSANNE (Switzerland).—Pop. 27,000. Situated on the northern bank of the Lake of Geneva. The Cathedral is the grandest Gothic structure in Switzerland. Vevey, Clarens, Castle of Chillon, Vernex, Montreux, etc., on the eastern shore of the Lake, may be easily visited from Ouchy, which is the port of Lausanne. A railway worked by hydraulic power connects Lausanne with Ouchy.

LUCERNE (Switzerland).—Pop. 14,000. Situated on the Lake of the Four Cantons and the River Reuss, commanding views of the Alps, including the Righi, Pilatus, etc. Places of interest:—Cathedral, Thorwaldsen's Lion; Glacier Garden; Stauffer's Museum; Covered bridges: old Roman watch-tower; Arsenal, etc. Steamers ply frequently between all the points of interest on the Lake.

MAYENCE (Germany).—Pop. 50,000. Situated at the junction of the River Main with the Rhine. Places of interest: Cathedral; Museum; Library; Picture Gallery; Roman Tower; Statues of Gutenberg and Schiller.

MILAN (Italy). Pop. 270,000. A convenient centre for tours in the Italian Lake district. Places of interest: - The Cathedral, the largest marble structure in the world (fine view from top of tower); Churches of St. Alessandro, St. Ambrogio, St. Maria delle Grazie, near which is the celebrated painting of "The Last Supper," by Leonardo da Vinci; the Galleria Vittorio Emanuele or public arcade; La Scala Theatre; Royal Palace; Brera; Arch of Peace, etc.

MUNICH (Bavaria). Pop. 170,000. Capital of Bavaria, is the headquarters of modern German art, and one of the most beautiful towns of Germany. There are several very fine churches: the Basilica of St. Boniface, in the Carlstrasse, is, without exception, the most beautiful church in Germany, in the Byzantine style. The Royal Palace consists of two parts, the old and new, a beautiful edifice after the model of the Pitti Palace in Florence, and rich in fresco paintings. The Colossal Statue of Bavaria and her Lion, half a mile from the Sendlinger Thor, is of copper, upwards of 60 feet high, on a pedestal of marble 40 feet high. A spiral staircase leads to the top; the head will hold eight persons, and there are holes to enable them to view the surrounding country. The Royal Library, a superb edifice in the Ludwig Strasse, with room enough to hold two millions of volumes, and in richness the second in the world; its Reading Room is open Monday. Wednesday and Friday. from 8 to 1 o'clock. The traveler should refer to the small daily German newspaper called the "Taglisher Anzeiger," for all particulars relating to Public Exhibitions and Amusements at Munich.

NAPLES (Italy).—Pop. 500,000. Situated in latitude 40° 52′ ; has a mean temperature of 60° 63° Fahr., the extreme heat of summer rarely attaining 100°, and the extreme cold in winter 28°. There are five principal entrances; that by the Bridge Della Maddalena near the Bay is the most striking; most of the houses are lofty and the streets narrow; there are, however, several open spaces of squares. The number of churches at Naples is about 330, and those best worth a visit are Gesu Nuovo, in the style of St. Peter's at Rome; the Sans Severo, a private chapel (remarkable statuary), San Francesco da Paolo; the Cathedral and the San Martino; St. Domenico Maggiore, San Severino e Soggia; La Incoronata; San Filippo Neri; San Lorenzo Maggiore; St. Maria del Carmine; all of them being adorned with pictures, etc., of the first masters. The National Museum will repay a good many visits, is possessing besides a picture gallery, the fresco paintings, mosaics, gold and silver ornaments, etruscan vases, etc., discovered in the excavations of Pompeii and Herculaneum. The Royal Library is annexed to the National Museum, and contains 250,000 volumes, besides more than 1,700 papyri, found in Herculaneum. The Albergo dei Poveri, an establishment for paupers and orphans, is worthy of a visit. It affords fixed relief to about 5,000 poor and pays the debts of deserving individuals. The environs abound with beauty and delightful reminiscences, including Virgil's Tomb, the Grotto of Posilippo, the Ruins of Pozznoli, Lake Avernus, and the classic shores of Bala and Misenum, the Islands of Ischia, Procida and Capri; the coast of Castellamare, the Orange Groves of Sorrento, Vesuvius, and the fields of lava; the streets of Pompeii, and the excavations of Herculaneum. The ascent of Vesuvius occupies about 8 hours; it is advisable to take refreshments with you, and to ride as far as the horses can go. Punta del Nasone, on Monte Somma, is 3,747 feet above the sea, but the highest point. Punta del Palo, is nearly 4,000 feet. The ruins of

Paestum may be visited in a day. Another delightful excursion is by railway to Castellamare (1 hour), and from thence to Sorrento, by carriage along the side of the Bay, one of the most beautiful drives in the world. English Church, Strada San Pasquale, at the back of the Riviera di Chiaja; the Rev. Pelham Maitland, M. A., is chaplain. Presbyterian church, 5, Capella Vecchia ; Minister, Rev. James Gordon Grey. Italian Evangelical Church and Schools, Palazzo Barbaia, No. 210 Toledo; Pastor, Rev. T. W. S. Jones, Wesleyan Missionary.

PARIS.—The capital of France. Pop. last census, 1,884,874. Principal public buildings and places of interest, with the hours at which they are open, are as follows :—

MUSEUMS.—The Louvre, every day except Monday, 10 a. m. to 4 p. m. Luxembourg, Sundays, 2 to 4 p. m.; other days, except Mondays, on production of passport, 11 a. m. to 4 p. m. Cluny (Boulevard St. Michel), daily on production of passport. Artillery Museum of the Invalides, Tuesday, Thursday and Sunday, 12 noon to 3 p. m. Depuytre (Ecole de Medicine), daily to students and medical men. Medailles (National Library), Tuesday, 11 a. m. to 3 p. m. Mineralogique (Boulevard St. Michel), Tuesday, Thursday and Saturday, 11 a. m. to 4 p. m. Museum of the Jardin des Plantes, Tuesday, Thursday and Saturday, by ticket.

CHURCHES.—La Madelaine, Notre Dame, St. Augustine, St. Eustache, St. Severin, St. Germain l'Auxerrois, St. Sulpice, St. Vincent de Paul, Larbonne, Chapelle Expiatoire de Louis XVI., all open daily; Sainte Chapelle, open daily, except Friday and Monday.

REMARKABLE BUILDINGS.—Hotel des Invalides, daily, 12 to 3. Tomb of Napoleon, Monday, Tuesday, Thursday, and Friday, 12 noon to 3 p. m. Hotel Dieu (Notre Dame), Thursday and Sunday ; Tour St. Jacques, daily ; Porte St. Denis ; Porte St. Martin; Pantheon, daily; Prisons of Mazas and La Roquette, by order of the Prefect of Police; Institute de France, daily, except Sundays; Imprimerie Nationale, by order of the Director ; National Library, daily, except Sunday; Mazarine Library, daily, from September to July; Ste. Genevieve Library, daily; National Archives, daily, except Sunday, 11 to 3 ; Bourse, daily, except Sunday; Gobelins, Wednesday and Saturday during summer; College de France, daily; Conservatoire des Arts, free on Sunday and Thursday, other days 1 franc.

THE PRINCIPAL STREETS AND THOROUGHFARES OF PARIS are the Champs Elysees, leading from the Tuileries Gardens to the Arc de Triomphe, which was built by Napoleon at a cost of £418,000 ; Bois de Boulogne, a public park laid out with great skill; Champ de Mars, a large open space facing the Military School.

THE PRINCIPAL BOULEVARDS are the Capucines, des Italiens, Montmartre, Poissonnier, St. Denis, St. Martin, du Prince Regent, Temple, Sebastopol and Strasbourg. The Rue de Rivoli and the Rue St. Honore are the main thoroughfares of the centre of the city.

PARIS is surrounded by fortifications 34,000 yards long. The city contains about 63,000 houses, 80 open spaces or squares, 27 bridges over the River Seine, 75 churches, 13 palaces, 35 theatres, 18 asylums or hospitals, 8 large public libraries, 6 lycees, and upwards of 2,000 schools and educational institutions.

The principal places of interest in the suburbs of Paris are :—St. Cloud (5 miles), reached by tram, railway, or steamer. St. Denis, where is the celebrated abbey church of St. Denis. Versailles (15 miles)—here is the magnificent Palace erected by Louis XIV. at a cost of £40,000,000. Sevres, the Government Porcelain Manufactory; St. Germain en Laye, with some pretty country scenery ; Fontainbleau (Forest and Park), 2 hours by rail, 16 trains a day.

PISA (Italy).—Pop. 26,000. One of the most ancient and beautiful cities of Italy. Situated on the Arno. The chief places of interest, besides the Cathedral, Baptistry, Leaning Tower and Campo Santo, are the church of St. Steven, in which are the remains of ships taken from the Turks in the 10th century, and more than 300 flags taken in Palestine in the 9th and 10th centuries, the

Pine Forests, 40 miles by 10, extending from Pisa to the sea, and stocked with every kind of selected game, as deer, wild boar, and pheasants. (Here there are a number of camels employed as beasts of burden.) Near Pisa (Viareggio) the poet Shelley was drowned. The interior of the Chartreuse, three-quarters of an hour from Pisa, is rich in pictures, marbles, and gardens. Half an hour's walk through a fine avenue of trees brings the visitor to the Spring of San Giuliano, esteemed by the Romans for its medicinal qualities. In addition, there are in or near Pisa, the churches of St. Catharine, S. Rattori, the Cascine, S. Rossore, and Gombo, a small bathing place. Lucca is half an hour and Leghorn twenty minutes by rail from Pisa.

ROME (the Capital of Italy)—(pop. 245,000)—is situated on the Tiber, partly on a plain and partly on low hills with their intersecting valleys, about 16 miles from the mouth of the river. Walls of 15 miles in circuit surround the entire city. The modern city is built upon the Campus Martius of the ancient Romans, lying along the banks of the Tiber, to the north of the seven hills, which formed the site of ancient Rome. There are 364 Churches; the principal ones are as follows:— St. Peter's, St. John Lateran, Santa Maria Maggiore, and Santa Croce in Gerusalemme, within the city; St. Paolo, San Lorenzo, and San Sebastian: the largest, St. Peter's, is built in form of a Latin cross. It occupied a period of 176 years in building, and required 350 years to perfect it, and cost £10,000,000; being kept in repair at a cost of £6,300 per annum. St. John Lateran is the Pope's Metropolitan church, he being its official minister. It is in this church also that the Popes were crowned. The Vatican stands prominent amongst the palaces here, and is the Winter Palace of the Pope, and stands over the Vatican Hill, near to St. Peter's. Here are also the Sixtine Chapel, and Vatican Library, containing the richest collection of manuscripts and pictures in the world. List of principal places and objects of interest in Rome:—The Palatine with Palace of the Cæsars; Basilica of Constantine; Arch of Titus; Temple of Venus and Rome; Domus Transitorio of Nero; Arch of Constantine; Meta Sudans; Colosseum: Lateran Museums;.Basilica of St. John Lateran; Scala Sancta; Aqueduct of Nero; Church of St. Stefano Rotondo, Temple of Vesta; Temple of Fortuna Virilis; Cloaca Maxima; Temples of Juno, Hope, and Piety; Theatre of Marcellus, Portico of Octavia; Forum Romanum; Mamertine Prison; Capitoline Museums: Tarpeian Rock: Fora of Trajan, Augustus, and Nerva; Golden House of Nero and Baths of Titus; Basilica of St. Clement; Basilica of St. Maria Maggiore; Church of Sta. Pudenziana: Vatican Museums; Sixtine Chapel; Stanze and Loggie of Raphael; Vatican Picture Gallery; St. Peter's, with ascent of Dome; the Pantheon; Basilica of Antoninus Pius; Antonine column; Janus Quadrifrons; Goldsmith's Arch; Circus Maximus; Baths of Caracalla: Tomb of the Scipios; Columbaria; Porta St. Sebastiano; Appian Way: Piazza Navona: Guard house of the VII. Cohort; Churches of Santa Maria in Trastevere; St. Maria in Via Lata; St. Maria degl' Angeli; St. Pietro in Vincoli; Monte Cavallo and Quirinal; Baths of Diocletian; Remains of the Agger of Servius Tullus; Church of St. Paul outside the Walls; Walls and Gates of Rome: Painted Tombs on the Via Latina. Palaces: —Quirinal, Doria, Colonna Orsini, Corsini, Spada, Barbarini, Farnese, Borghese, Farnesina, &c., &c. Outside the walls excursions may be made to Ostia, Villa Hadrian, Tivoli, Frascati, &c. Cook's Tourist office, 1 B Piazza di Spagna.

ROTTERDAM (Holland).—Pop. 129,000. Large commercial city. Places of interest:- Cathedral, Old Church, South Church, Town Hall, Exchange, Botanical Gardens, Boyman's Museum, Groote Kerk, Market, &c.

STRASBOURG (Alsace).—Pop. 82,000. Taken from the French in 1870. Places of interest:- Cathedral, one of the finest in the world, containing the famous clock; statue of Guttenberg. The ascent of the Cathedral tower should be made to obtain a view of the surrounding country.

TURIN (Italy).—Pop. 212,000. Places of interest:—Royal Palace, Churches of St. John the Baptist, St. Filippe Neri and St. Lorenzo; University; Royal Academy of Science; Academy of Arts, Egyptian Museum ; Armory Museum:

Civic Museum; Palazzo Madama, etc. The Church of Superga, 5 miles from Turin, contains the Mausoleum of the Royal Family.

VENICE (Italy)—(pop. 129,000)—is built on 72 islands, on piles, in the midst of a salt lagoon, or shallow lake. It is divided into two parts by the Grand Canal, the course of which flows through the city in the form of an inverted S, is 330 feet wide, crossed near the middle of its course by the Ponte di Rialto, a splendid marble structure of one spacious arch. In the midst of the labyrinth of canals and streets there are several large Piazzas, nearly all of which are adorned with fine churches or palaces. The principal of these is the Piazza di San Marco, a large oblong area 562 feet by 232, surrounded by elegant buildings, and containing at its extremity the Church of San Marco; a singular but brilliant combination of the Gothic and the Oriental styles of architecture. In the Piazza is the Campanile, 316 feet high and 42 feet square, with a pyramidal top, to which the ascent is made by an inclined plane. Adjoining the Church are the ancient palace of the Doges, the prisons, and other public offices of the late Venetian Republic. San Marco was founded in the year 828, by the Doge Guistiniano Participazio, for the purpose of receiving the relics of St. Mark. Principal places of interest:—Cathedral, Churches of St. Maria della Salute, St. Giorgio Maggiore, Frari Scalzi, S. Salvatore, St. Sebastiano, St. Redentore, S. Rocco, S. Senola, S. Pantaleone, S. Maria Carmine, S. Trovaso, S. Stefano, S. Zobenigo, S. Moise, S. Zanipolo, Jesuits, Madonna dell' Orto; Academy of Fine Arts; Doge's Palace; Royal Palace; Armenian Convent on the Lido, etc.

VERONA (Italy).—Pop. 60,000. Situated at the base of the Alps, on the river Adige. One of the most important fortified towns of northern Italy. Places of interest:—The Arena; Piazza del Signori; Palazzo del Consiglio; Tombs of the Scalligeri; Cathedral, etc.

ZURICH (Switzerland).—Pop. 21,199. The capital of the Canton, situated on the north end of the Lake of Zurich, and on the banks of the river Limmat, and is one of the most flourishing manufacturing Swiss towns. Places of interest:—Town Library; Grossmunster; Cloisters; Town Hall, and Hohe Promenade.

☞ *For a full description of the above places, the Traveler will do well to consult Cook's Tourist Guide Books, a list of which will be found on second page of cover of this pamphlet.*

COOK'S
Excursions, Tours and General Traveling Arrangements.

THOMAS COOK & SON, 261 Broadway, New York,
(Chief Office, Ludgate Circus, London).

ORIGINATORS OF THE TOURIST AND EXCURSION SYSTEM
(Established 1841).
And ONLY Successful Conductors of Tours and Excursions to all parts of the Globe.

Specially appointed by his Royal Highness the Prince of Wales Sole Passenger Agents to the Royal British Commission, Vienna, 1873; Philadelphia, 1876; Paris, 1878; also Agents by appointment to the Brussels and Dusseldorf Exhibition Administrations, 1880. Officially appointed by the Italian Government Administration Sole Agents for International Passenger Traffic over the State Railways of Italy. Sole Managing Agents for the Khedive Mail Steamers from Cairo to the First and Second Cataracts—the only Steamers on the Nile. General Passenger Agents in America for the Midland Railway of England, &c., &c.

PIONEERS, INAUGURATORS AND PROMOTERS OF THE PRINCIPAL SYSTEM OF TOURS ESTABLISHED IN ALL PARTS OF THE GLOBE.

THOS. COOK & SON are now giving **increased attention** to ordinary TRAVELING ARRANGEMENTS, with a view to rendering it **Easy, Practicable and Economical.** During the past forty years more than **6 Millions** of travelers near and distant points under their management, safely and pleasantly. Their arrangements are now so extensive that they cover portions of the four quarters of the Globe. At their office in New York can be found the Railway and Steamship Tickets used by the travelers for a journey through all parts of

IRELAND, SCOTLAND, ENGLAND, WALES, FRANCE, GERMANY, BAVARIA, AUSTRIA,
Holland, Belgium, Spain, Portugal, Italy, Turkey, Cyprus, Egypt, Greece, The Levant, Palestine, India, China, Australia, New Zealand, &c.

COOK'S IRISH TOURS.—Messrs. Thos. Cook & Son issue Tourist Tickets to and through all parts of Ireland, available for the passenger to land at Londonderry, Belfast or Queenstown going, or to embark at those places returning; and enabling him to visit the Giant's Causeway, Belfast, Dublin, Galway, Loch Erne, the Lakes of Killarney, etc. They can be used to those places alone, or can be combined with Tours to any other country, and issued by any line of Steamers.

COOK'S SCOTCH TOURS cover all points of Tourist interest in Scotland; including Oban, Staffa, Iona, Isle of Skye, Caledonian Canal, Kyles of Bute, the Trossachs, the Highlands, the Lake District, Edinburgh, etc., and can be used in a similar manner to the Irish Tours.

COOK'S ENGLISH TOURS.—Messrs. Cook & Son issue Midland Railway Tickets from Glasgow or Liverpool to London, or return from London to those points, embracing all the noted places like Melrose, Abbotsford, Chatsworth, Haddon Hall, the Derbyshire Peak District, etc., which will allow the passenger to break his journey at pleasure. New arrangements have also been made for Tours to all parts of interest in the English Lake District. Tickets are also issued from Liverpool to London by the Great Western Railway, allowing breaks of journey at all principal points en route.

COOK'S WEST OF ENGLAND TOURS, combining Railway, Coach and Steamer to every point of interest between Bristol and the Land's End. The tickets are prepared in the Coupon form, and can be issued in combination to meet the requirements of the Tourist.

COOK'S TOURS TO HOLLAND, BELGIUM AND THE RHINE are available for all lines from New York and London, for a single journey or a return journey; they are the only tickets permitting their holders to stop at their convenience at such interesting places as Rotterdam, Amsterdam, Antwerp, Brussels, Aix-la-Chapelle, Cologne, Bonn, Coblentz, Bingen, Mayence, Worms, Heidelberg, Baden-Baden, etc.

COOK'S SWISS TOURS.—Switzerland has been completely covered with their Tourist arrangements; every Alpine pass and route is shown in their programmes.

COOK'S ITALIAN TOURS are over one hundred in number, combining every country with Italy; going via Paris and Mont Cenis, Switzerland, and any of the Passes, the South of France, the Rhine, Bavaria, and Semmering; and all the tickets shown are at reductions ranging from thirty to forty-five per cent. below ordinary fares.

NORWAY, SWEDEN AND DENMARK.—Messrs. Thos. Cook & Son issue Tourist Tickets by all principal Railways and Steamers for the most interesting parts of Scandinavia.

ALGERIAN TOURS.—Messrs. Thos. Cook & Son issue Tickets by any route to Algeria, and over the Algerian Railways and Diligences.

TURKEY, CYPRUS, GREECE, THE LEVANT, &c.—Messrs. Thos. Cook & Son are now prepared to issue Tickets by any line of Steamers to any port touched by the

Austrian Lloyd's, Messageries Maritimes, Rubattino, Russian, Khedivic Mail and other Company's Steamers.

TOURS TO PALESTINE are rendered easy, safe and economical by the superior arrangements of Messrs. Thos. Cook & Son, who have their own Resident Manager in Beyrout and Jaffa. They are therefore prepared to conduct large or small parties in the most comfortable manner through the country; to Jerusalem, the Dead Sea, the Jordan, Damascus, Sinai, &c. Small parties can be so fixed as to go independently or under personal management any time between October and April. Over two thousand ladies and gentlemen have visited Palestine under their arrangements.

THE STEAM NAVIGATION OF THE NILE is committed by the Khedive Government entirely to Messrs. Thos. Cook & Son. The Steamers (the only ones on the Nile) ply between Cairo and the First Cataract (600 miles), and the Second Cataract (810 miles). Tickets can be had and berths secured at any of Messrs. Thos. Cook & Son's Offices.

MIDLAND RAILWAY.—Messrs. Thos. Cook & Son are the American General Passenger Agents for the Midland Railway of England. This Railway is equipped with Pullman Drawing-Room, Parlor and Sleeping Cars, which are run on all trains between London, Liverpool and Glasgow.

PERSONALLY-CONDUCTED PARTIES are constantly being organized, leaving New York and London for certain definite and prescribed Tours, for which one sum is quoted, which includes all expenses necessary for the Tour—Steamers, Railways, Hotels, Omnibuses, etc.

TO PARIS AND BACK.—Messrs. Thos. Cook & Son have prepared a series of Tours to Paris and return by all lines of Steamers at the lowest rates, and have made special arrangements in Paris for the reception of American tourists. For full information consult COOK'S EXCURSIONIST.

INDIA, CHINA, JAPAN, AUSTRALIA, &c.—Messrs. Thos. Cook & Son are the American Agents for the Peninsular and Oriental Steam Navigation Co., and of the principal Steamship Companies of the world, and are prepared to issue tickets from Southampton, Venice, Ancona and Brindisi to Alexandria, Aden, Bombay, Calcutta, Singapore, Hong Kong, Shanghai, or any other point in India, China or Japan, also to King G's Sound, Melbourne and Sydney.

AUSTRALASIAN TOURS.—Messrs. Thos. Cook & Son, under special contracts with the Colonial Government Railway Administration, issue tickets over all the Railways in Australia and New Zealand, at greatly reduced fares.

AMERICAN TOURS.—Messrs. Thos. Cook & Son have their own system of Tours in America, covering all points of interest between the Atlantic and Pacific Oceans.

ROUND THE WORLD.—Messrs. Thos. Cook & Son are now prepared to issue a direct traveling ticket for a journey Round the World by Steam, commencing in New York, Chicago or San Francisco, and ending at any of those places, available to go either West or East.

COOK'S HOTEL COUPONS, available at nearly five hundred first-class hotels in various parts of the world, can be had by travelers purchasing Cook's Tourist Tickets, guaranteeing them first-class accommodation at fixed and regular prices.

THOS. COOK & SON'S GENERAL TRAVELING ARRANGEMENTS are so widely extended that they can supply tickets to almost any point that Tourists may wish to visit, in many cases at reductions from ordinary fares. The regular traveling ticket being issued in all cases, printed in English on one side and the language of the country where it is used on the other, and containing all the information the traveler needs. Those contemplating a Tour need only call on Thos. Cook & Son, 261 Broadway, New York, giving the journey they propose, when the price of their tickets will be at once quoted.

THE GUIDE BOOKS published by Messrs. Thos. Cook & Son are both practical and concise. A list of them can be obtained on application, or will be found in the EXCURSIONIST.

COOK'S EXCURSIONIST is published monthly in New York, at ten cents per copy, or one dollar per annum, and contains programmes of nearly one thousand specimen Tours, tickets for which are issued by Messrs. Thos. Cook & Son, with fares by every Line of Steamers leaving New York. The EXCURSIONIST can be had by mail, postpaid, upon application.

Another edition of the EXCURSIONIST is published in London, and an edition in the French language is published in Paris and Brussels every month.

For further particulars apply to **THOS. COOK & SON'S TOURIST OFFICES.**

NEW YORK, 261 Broadway.	LEEDS, 1 Royal Exchange.	NAPLES, Sommer's Fine Art Gal.
BOSTON, 197 Washington Street.	SHEFFIELD, Change Alley Cor.	MALTA, 280 Strada Reale, Valetta.
PHILADELPHIA, 1351 Chestnut Street.	NOTTINGHAM, 16 Clumber St.	ALGIERS, 27 & 28, Rampe Chasseloup Laubat.
WASHINGTON, 1431 Pennsylvania Avenue.	MANCHESTER, 61 Market Street.	CAIRO, (EGYPT,) Cook's Pavillion.
	WALSALL, P. O. Building, the Bridge.	
CHICAGO, Sherman House.	BIRMINGHAM, Stephenson Place.	ALEXANDRIA, Hotel Europe.
TORONTO, 35 Yonge Street.	WOLVERHAMPTON, 27 Queen St.	JAFFA, PALESTINE, Jerusalem Hotel.
NEW ORLEANS, 35 Carondelet St.	LEICESTER, 5½ Gallowtree Gate.	
LONDON, Ludgate Circus, Fleet Street.	PARIS, 15 Place du Havre.	CHIEF OFFICE FOR INDIA, 5 Hornby Row, Bombay.
LIVERPOOL, 11 Ranelagh Street.	BRUSSELS, 22 Galerie du Roi.	CHIEF AUSTRALASIAN OFFICE The Exchange, Melbourne.
GLASGOW, 165 Buchanan Street.	COLOGNE, 49 Domhof.	
EDINBURGH, 9 Princes Street.	GENEVA, 30 Rue du Rhone.	NEW ZEALAND AGENCY, Auckland.
DUBLIN, 45 Dame Street.	ROME, 1 il Piazza di Spagna.	
BRADFORD, 8 Exch. Market St.	NICE, Grand Hotel.	

All communications respecting European, Eastern and American Tours and Excursions to be addressed to

THOS. COOK & SON, Chief American Office, 261 Broadway, New York, P. O. Box 4197.

Manager of the American Business, C. A. BARATTONI. Or any of their authorized Offices or Agencies.

AMERICAN EXCHANGE IN EUROPE,
(LIMITED).

CAPITAL, - - ONE MILLION DOLLARS.

President—JOSEPH R. HAWLEY.
General Manager—HENRY F. GILLIG.

No. 449 STRAND, LONDON, W. C.

HEADQUARTERS for AMERICANS in EUROPE.

FREEDOM OF EXCHANGE AND READING ROOMS:

Per month..........5s. or $1.25 | Per annum..........£2 or $10.00

The freedom of the EXCHANGE and READING ROOMS carries with it the following advantages:—

(*a.*) The use of the largest number of American newspapers—daily, weekly, religious, scientific, pictorial, and sporting—on file anywhere in Europe.

(*b.*) The use of the largest number of guide-books, maps, charts, gazetteers, magazines, and other publications, official or non-official, of interest to tourists, to be found in any institution of the kind in any country.

(*c.*) The use of the only place in Europe where the Directories of American cities and towns are kept.

(*d.*) The use of the only place in London where arrivals are registered, published weekly and circulated throughout the world.

(*e.*) The use of the only place where travelers can obtain their letters and telegraphic messages **every day** and **hour** throughout the year. (This is of vital importance to persons arriving by evening trains and leaving London the following day, and also to all persons sailing on the day following any holiday.)

(*f.*) The only place in London where Americans can get their drafts cashed on English bank holidays. Travelers have saved steamers that they would have lost in the absence of this facility.

(*g.*) The use of the only place where the arrival of steamers on both sides of the Atlantic is made known by telegraph immediately on being signaled.

(*h.*) The only place where passenger lists of all in-coming and out-going Atlantic steamers are kept on file.

(*i.*) The use of the only place of the kind where there is a separate reading and writing-room for ladies.

The freedom of the EXCHANGE and READING ROOMS includes the care and re-mailing of letters, telegrams, etc., and the exclusive use of a P. O. Box.

Yale Lock P. O. Boxes and Private Drawers and Desks may be had when desired, also use of the Committee Room for Board Meetings or other special purposes.

TRAVELERS' BAGGAGE stored at the express and storage department, 3 Adelaide Street, Charing Cross.

The Principal American Newspapers and Guide Books on Sale.

Over 600 Newspapers, 200 City and State Directories, 300 Official, State, and Municipal Reports, regularly filed in the Reading Rooms of the Exchange.

TRAVELERS' BRANCH OPEN DAILY FROM NINE A. M. TO MIDNIGHT.

Printed addressed envelopes free of cost can be obtained of THE PRINCIPAL BANKS, HOTELS, AND STEAMSHIP OFFICES, and at the Chief American Office of Messrs. THOS. COOK & SON, 261 Broadway, New York, or any of their authorized Agencies in America.